SOTHIS PRESS

Sothis Press aims to completely reimagine the public domain book with an emphasis on universal access to captivatingly designed print editions. We believe that technology will enable every single book ever published to be perpetually accessible in beautiful print form. Sothis is beauty in ubiquity.

www.sothis.press
1 Waterhouse Square, London, ECIN 2ST

The Story of Camp Ellis

Robert O. Burton

SOTHIS PRESS

ISBN 978-1-83548-636-8

This edition is published by
Sothis Press © 2023. The company
is registered in England and Wales.
The Company Number is 14900389.

Foreword . . .

THIS book was planned to present, in words and pictures, the story of Camp Ellis. Though its history is brief in relation to time, its importance cannot be acknowledged until the war is won. We will venture a guess that destiny will pay its rightful tribute.

This story is dedicated to the American soldier; the courageous living and the honored dead. Reflected in these pages is the natural pride we take in the Ellis-trained units that are writing the close of this history in scores of battle areas.

We have endeavored to be readable and authentic, including as many pictures as were available for the space. The text, of necessity, has been limited to an outline story of the Camp from its inception to the reports of Ellis-trained units overseas. Official War Department records, week to week accounts of camp events as recorded in the Camp Ellis News, group and unit histories prepared especially for the Historical Research Section, were the main sources of information for this book. Some outstanding records of accomplishments were omitted for security reasons.

Much is still to be written to complete the story. These chapters, in many instances, are being inscribed in sweat and blood wherever the men of Camp Ellis are serving and fighting for victory. Every American is proud of the achievements of our Army, and if, in the case of the individual, unsung soldier, this book adds to that pride, its purpose will have been fulfilled.

Sergeant Michael B. Ellis

DOUGHBOYS called him "The Lone Wolf." Newspapers described him as the "Sergeant York of St. Louis." Radio announcers introduced him as "Machine-gun Mike." But on Army records he was plain Sergeant Michael Ellis of St. Louis, possessor of the Congressional Medal of Honor and the Silver Star.

This camp was officially named in his honor approximately 26 years after Sergeant Ellis performed the dangerous missions that made him a national hero. His deeds closely paralleled those of Sergeant York.

Fighting was bitter in the Argonne sector that damp, dreary day in the autumn of '18. Ellis' outfit, the famous First Division, was in the thick of the raging battle. During the engagement, Sergeant Ellis operated far in advance of the first wave of his company, voluntarily undertaking the most dangerous missions, single-handedly attacking machine-gun nests. Flanking one emplacement, he killed two of the enemy with rifle fire and captured 27 prisoners, including two officers and six machine-guns which had been holding up the advance of his company. The captured officers indicated the location of the other four machine-guns and Ellis in turn captured these, together with their crews.

The distinguished soldier was born in St. Louis on October 28, 1894. His mother died when he was an infant, and his father was too poor to provide for him properly. Little Michael was adopted by a Polish family who lived in East St. Louis, Ill. When he was 12, he quit school and went to work in his foster father's printing plant. After four years a more exciting sort of life beckoned. He wanted to be a soldier, and he could think and talk of nothing else. His father witnessed his under-age enlistment at Jefferson Barracks, Missouri, on February 8, 1912.

He saw service with Company K, 7th Infantry, along the Mexican border and at Vera Cruz. When his three years were up, Ellis received his honorable discharge, but after six months of civilian life he re-enlisted. He was promoted to corporal on April 16, 1917, and to sergeant a month later. After many memorable campaigns throughout France, battles in which Ellis displayed amazing valor and ingenuity while utterly disregarding his personal safety, he was promoted to first sergeant. As a private in Company C, 28th Infantry, 1st Division, he saw front-line action for 200 days near Soissons, France. He was awarded the Silver Star. The official record of the War Department states: "He showed unusual courage in carrying supplies and in attacking strong points at Brouil, Pleissy, and Berney-le-Sac." Our allies, recognizing Sergeant Ellis' bravery, awarded him the Chevalier Legion of Honor of France, and the Croix-de-Guerre with Palm, the Cross of War of Italy, Cross of War of Poland and Recognition by the Moroccan Government, two medals, Senior and Junior.

In August, 1919, Sergeant Ellis returned to the United States and St. Louis, where General Pershing presented him with the Congressional Medal of Honor. He was the only soldier in Pershing's First Division to receive this honor. He was feted and toasted for his gallant deeds, but later, when he sought civilian employment, it was not to be had. Informed of his status, President Coolidge provided for Ellis' employment at the Post Office in St. Louis.

On January 2, 1921 he met a bright-eyed, attractive young woman of Polish descent. They discovered they had been childhood playmates in East St. Louis; they had many memories of mutual interest. Thus began a post-war romance that culminated in marriage on February 13, 1923, in St. Louis.

Sergeant Ellis died of pneumonia in a Chicago hospital on December 9, 1937. He was buried with full military honors in Arlington National Cemetery.

William Walters purchasing Bernadotte from the Indians in 1826.

Bernadotte

A PICTURESQUE pioneer village snuggled between green hills and oak woods, through which the drowsy Spoon River wended its way—that was Bernadotte in the peaceful pre-war days. Its demise was undreamed of then by the tiny population which tilled its rich soil and fished its historic river. The ominous war clouds which hung over foreign lands were thousands of miles away and not even the most visionary native could forsee the far-reaching effects of the inevitable cloudburst. To most it seemed unreal that the peaceful village of Bernadotte reclining on the banks of the Spoon River in the heart of Illinois would feel the effects of a war two oceans away.

Then it happened. The whole world heard the thunderous burst and was stunned. America was mobilizing. Camps were springing up in every section of the country. A huge military encampment was planned for Illinois and in a section of the 17,800-acre tract selected lay Bernadotte. A war casualty, Bernadotte and its place on the American scene as a pioneering Mid-western community will never be forgotten.

Henry Zoll's grist mill and the old dam, from an early picture.

Bernadotte Schoolhouse.

Immortalized and called the "Village of Seven Hills" by Edgar Lee Masters in his world-famous "Spoon River Anthology," Bernadotte, states legend, was bought from the Indians in 1826 by William Walters, an Indian fighter who paid only 50 deer skins for the village.

At first the community was called Fulton. No suitable explanation can be found for this name but it was probably because the village was located in Fulton County. After a visit to the community by John Baptiste Jules Barnadotte, a French general and favorite of Napoleon who was attracted to the village by the beauty of its hills, the villagers, so impressed and flattered by this unprecedented visit of royalty, changed the name to Barnadotte. It later became Bernadotte and no reason has been found for this revision.

In its pioneering days Bernadotte developed an unenviable reputation as a rough town. It was notorious for its lawlessness and tough characters who almost daily were hauled into court on assault and murder charges. Masters, in his book "The Sangamon," describes numerous incidents

which branded the knife, pistol and brassknuck-carrying toughs as notorious. He tells of one of the terrible toughs of Bernadotte who came one day to Marietta in Harris Township to kill a doctor. The doctor's son stepped to the sidewalk when he saw the wild man approaching and blew him to pieces with a blast from a shotgun.

Despite these frequent disorders, life in Bernadotte was simple. A flour mill on the Spoon River was the center of business activity, although a good portion of the village income was derived from its one fishing and two packing plants and from the patronage of summer tourists. In addition, the soil was productive and the timber strong.

But it was around the grist mill, which was to be made famous by the writings of Masters, that Bernadotte life revolved. Farmers came to the mill with their wheat and corn. Most of them came from Laurel Hill, now known as Table Grove, and Ipava, recalled by old-timers as Pleasantville. The grist mill was owned by Henry Zoll and served the entire community. He got his waterpower from a dam. Another dam, 12 miles below at Babylon, made the narrow, winding river navigable, which favored a thriving and prosperous river traffic. Bernadotte's future seemed assured.

Then the railroad came, but Bernadotte was not to share its advantages. Instead, the importance of Bernadotte was dwarfed by the railroads. Barge traffic ended on the Spoon. The mill trade was diverted elsewhere and Henry Zoll's business slackened. Bernadotte, once a reckless, lawless community; later a peaceful, active and prosperous village, started to fade. Its population of over 500, a "big" for those days, dwindled.

War and Camp Ellis came. Their arrival signaled the end of Bernadotte. The handful of families in the village bade it farewell. Its grist mill, dilapidated and tottering, was razed. Homes and farm buildings were torn down.

Where once crops grew, villagers congregated, youngsters romped, business stirred and ruffians fought, the monotonous tramp of marching feet was heard.

Bernadotte is gone and all that remains is a little red brick schoolhouse, a framework of an old house—and a pleasant memory.

Construction

ACRES of tall corn were swaying in the breeze of an Illinois September, in 1942, when heavy Army tractors and equipment rolled over the fertile soil and began the transformation of endless cornfields and farmland into a busy military city. It was on the 17th day of that September when native farmers, who for years had tilled their lands, stood by and watched their peaceful fields shudder and burst open under the impact of the engineering machinery which scraped, dug and twisted their land into an unrecognizable tract.

The arrival of equipment signalled the beginning of a gigantic construction job. The important preliminaries, however, had begun in the early fall of 1941. At that time, aerial surveys were made of the flat terrain of Fulton County for the selection of the site on which the cantonment was to be built. Plans then tentatively called for Ellis to accommodate a full division. Shortly afterwards, in December, countless stakes were pounded into the soft earth in the Table Grove-Ipava area and hundreds of plans were drawn up and studied. All this represented thousands of hours of work under the supervision of Capt. R. K. Sawyer, area engineer, during the planning of the camp from December, 1941, until June, 1942. Nine days before construction began Major K. M. Pattee arrived on War Department orders to supervise the project, replacing Capt. Sawyer who had completed his task.

That was the picture on September 17, 1942, when construction began on what later was to grow into one of the largest Army Service Forces training camps in the country. Originally planned for 75,000 acres, the size of the camp was later reduced to 17,750 acres.

Work was begun on a railroad track between the camp and Table Grove. Makeshift roads were dug out of the soft earth. Ditches and excavation work marked the final location of water lines, sewer lines and buildings. Fleets of trucks snaked along narrow dirt roads carrying materials and workers.

An ironical picture presented itself with the arrival in Fulton County of thousands of workers. As they streamed in from all sections of Illinois, there was an exodus of farmers and their families from the land taken over by the government. It was a sad departure for the many who left homes and farms which had been owned by their kin for generations.

Construction was in its early stages when bad weather set in, becoming an exasperating enemy. Snow started to fall and the freshly-turned soil received its first winter coat. Roads resembled dirty rivers. The ground hardened. Batches of concrete froze before they were poured, and sometimes for days, construction was at a standstill. Slowly the obstacles were overcome and out of the frozen earth sprung building after building. Where only a few months before stood cornfields, dim outlines of Camp Ellis now appeared.

As the buildings began to mushroom, it was observed that virtually all of them were one-story frame structures, and not the two-story buildings found in most camps. Because of a shortage of critical materials, wall boards, and manufactured siding were substituted on roofs and walls of the buildings. Late winter found the construction ahead of schedule, water flowing through the water mains, the electrical distribution section in operation, roads and sidewalks growing out of mud ruts. The Area Engineer formally transferred the first building—a warehouse—to the jurisdiction of the post on March 24.

Approximately six months after construction got underway—April 15, 1943—Pattee, then a lieutenant-colonel, turned over the keys of Camp Ellis to Col. Basil D. Spalding, Commanding Officer.

This marked the official opening of Camp Ellis—one month ahead of schedule. Newspapermen taken on a tour of the camp saw a streamlined military city of one-story barracks, complete water and drainage system, fire department, modern hospital, warehouses, recreational facilities, and a prisoner of war camp. Construction of the camp was completed under the most adverse weather conditions. Handicapped not only by inclement weather, but also by material and labor shortages, gasoline and other wartime shortages, the contractors with tireless crews worked hard and long to complete their mission. To them must go much credit.

Colonel Basil D. Spalding

Organized Army Service Forces Unit Training Center in Chicago and assumed command in February, 1943 . . . transferred Training Center Headquarters to Camp Ellis in following April and became first commanding officer . . . has more than 30 years service . . . was with Company K, 20th Infantry from 1914 to 1916 and held grades of private, corporal, sergeant and first sergeant . . . was commissioned second lieutenant of infantry in 1916 and advanced to captain during World War I . . . saw service on Mexican Border . . . was decorated with Silver Star with Oak Leaf Cluster and Purple Heart in World War 1 . . . is a graduate of the Command and General Staff School, the Infantry School and the Army War College . . . served as Training Group Commander and later as Director of Training at Camp Ellis under General Maxwell, second camp commander.

Major General Russell L. Maxwell

Born in Oakdale, Illinois, approximately 200 miles south of Camp Ellis . . . took command of Camp Ellis on May 1, 1943 . . . was graduated from West Point in 1912 . . . served in Hawaii as artillery officer . . . commanded Army's largest powder-manufacturing arsenal in World War I . . . served in Army of Occupation in Rhineland . . . commanded ordnance depot near Coblenz, Germany . . . was member of staff of Assistant Secretary of War for two years . . . appointed a colonel in 1940 and assigned by President Roosevelt to post of Administrator of Export Control . . . was appointed chief of the U. S. Military North Africa Mission in 1941 . . . mission assisted British forces in Middle East and set up air and naval installations in Eritrea and shop installations in Egypt, Palestine and Libya . . . promoted to Brigadier-General in January, 1941, and to Major-General in March, 1942.

Brigadier General George E. Hartman

Third commanding officer of Camp Ellis . . . took command on October 5, 1943, and served until December 18, 1943 . . . native of Brookhaven, Miss. . . . veteran of 27 years of Army service . . . commissioned first lieutenant in Mississippi National Guard in 1917 . . . saw action in World War I as artillery officer . . . commanded installations at Honolulu and in the Philippines . . . supervised new construction at Fort Francis E. Warren, Wyo. in 1940 . . . instrumental in organizing first Quartermaster Replacement Training Center in 1941 . . . elevated to full colonel in December of 1941 . . . organized Quartermaster Unit Training Center at Vancouver Barracks, Washington, in 1942 . . . arrived at Camp Ellis in April, 1943 . . . promoted to brigadier-general the following month . . . served as Quartermaster Group commander and inspector of Army Service Forces Unit Training Center.

Colonel John S. Sullivan

A native of Louisiana . . . graduated from West Point, Class of 1907 with Bachelor of Science degree . . . was the fourth camp commander . . . assumed command on December 18, 1943 . . . held temporary rank of lieutenant-colonel in Air Service during World War I . . . reverted to permanent rank of captain in the infantry at the end of the war . . . earned permanent promotion to major in 1920, lieutenant-colonel in 1931 and colonel in 1936 . . . commanded Fort Clayton and 33rd Infantry in the Panama Canal Zone before going to Chicago in 1939 . . . served as director of Civilian Component Affairs for Sixth Corps Area in Chicago . . . became director of Personnel Division . . . later became Deputy Chief of Staff of the Sixth Service Command . . . graduate of Army Command and General Staff School at Ft. Leavenworth, Kansas . . . under his command Camp Ellis reached its maximum strength.

Governor Dwight H. Green delivering dedicatory address.

Dedication Day

ON JULY 4, 1943, 50,000 natives of Illinois streamed into Camp Ellis to witness one of the largest and most colorful events ever staged in Central Illinois. The occasion was the formal dedication of Camp Ellis. Despite the threat held by gloomy skies they came from cities, farms and rural sections to behold their new streamlined military city, its population and its war activities. What these people saw amazed them.

They saw thousands of men preparing for the grim adventures of war. They saw these men crawl over infiltration courses while machine-gun bullets spattered overhead . . . they saw these men run the difficult obstacle course... they saw signalmen administer first aid at the top of a telephone pole . . . engineers demonstrate pontoon bridges, assault boats and booby traps . . . they saw bread baked in field ovens . . . they saw mobile laundry units in action... hospital tents, sanitary areas, gas mask drills . . . they saw engineer, medical, quartermaster and service troops toiling in jobs that in the near future they would be undertaking in combat areas.

They saw rows and rows of one-story buildings where men lived, ate and played . . . they visited GI' "5 and 10" stores, chapels, recreation halls, theaters, mess halls, service clubs, warehouses, and administration buildings.

They saw the unveiling of a portrait of Sergeant Michael Ellis, St. Louis youth whose valor in World War I won for him the Congressional Medal of Honor and for whom Camp Ellis was named . . . they saw five Ellis soldiers decorated for heroism . . . they saw a Peoria girl, Miss Esther Ready, crowned Dedication Day queen . . . they saw thousands of soldiers smartly pass in review . . . they rode in Army jeeps and trucks . . . they walked around the green hills and along the Spoon River, where once stood the pioneer village of Bernadotte.

And as the program neared its climax, they were greeted by the first citizen of their state, the Hon. Dwight H. Green, Governor of Illinois. In his eloquent way he welcomed both the Army to its new training center in the heart of the Prairie State, and its citizens to witness the scope of training being conducted in this military city which many of them had physically helped to provide and to which all were patriotically contributing.

In closing, Major General Russell L. Maxwell, the camp commander, brought to focus the purpose of this tremendous program, dedicating these accumulated facilities to the goal of the best of training for the finest of men for the greatest good.

Ellis men parade . . .

. . . to martial music.

Visitors examine displays.

Dedication Day crowd.

Headquarters

THE life-line of an Army camp is its headquarters . From it stems the machinery of organization linking it to the lower echelons of command.

The following chapter traces the history of the Headquarters of Camp Ellis from the time it merely existed on paper through its two years of development and growth. Closely allied with the mechanical functions of Headquarters were the policies of the four commanding officers whose foresight, ingenuity and perseverence contributed personal elements to the general panorama of command.

The story of the Station Hospital and the Prisoners of War Camp, although parts of Headquarters, are described in separate sections of this chapter.

Gen. Maxwell receives command from Col. Spalding.

Headquarters

IN EARLY 1942, shortly after the United States was plunged into World War II by the sneak Japanese raid on Pearl Harbor, the War Department set machinery in motion to establish a training camp somewhere in Illinois. The Sixth Service Command sent a board of officers, all specialists in camp planning, to select possible sites for construction.

Three locations were selected and Washington sent its representatives to Illinois to make a final decision. The area now known as Camp Ellis was chosen and designated as the Lewistown Project. This area was picked over the others mainly because of its nearness to Galesburg, an important railroad center with east-west rail connections.

War Department changes called for a revision of the original plan and instead of an infantry camp the Lewistown Project was picked to come under the jurisdiction of the Services of Supply as a new type unit training center. Representatives of the Service Command, Col. Basil D. Spalding and Lt. Col. Fred W. Wolter, who worked on the original plan, met with Services of Supply Training Officers in Washington in December, 1942. At this meeting the final plan of organization was drafted. Construction of the camp, which had started before this meeting, was well underway.

On Jan. 31, 1943, Camp Ellis was activated and Col. Basil D. Spalding, a regular Army officer, who was on the board of officers who assisted in selecting the site and worked on the original plans, was named commanding officer.

Col. Spalding issued general order No. 2 Feb. 15, 1943, announcing the first seven appointments to his headquarters staff. They were: Col. Hans C. Minuth, executive officer; Lt. Col. Fred W. Wolter, chief of the personnel branch; Lt. Col. Dallas G. Warne, chief of supply and service branch; Lt. Col. Randolph F. Olmsted, camp surgeon; Maj. John C. Evans, Internal Security Officer; Lt. Thomas K. Blender, Public Relations Officer; and Lt. Glen A. Trevor, Intelligence Officer.

While these staff members were handling the preliminaries and conducting their paper work from the Chicago office, other officers were ordered to Ellis to assist in the camp's on-the-spot organization and construction. Before their departure, Col. Spalding called a special meeting and explained that Camp Ellis was being established as a unit training center for approximately 35,000 men, with compound facilities for 3,000 prisoners of war. The mission of the new encampment, he stated, was to activate and train supply units capable of functioning as supporting troops in theaters of operations or in zones of interior.

Lt. Col. Robert C. Edgar, the Post Engineer, arrived here on March 20, with orders to prepare the camp for occupancy on April 15. He was followed by Capt. Anson M. Aikman, Quartermaster representative assigned to receive and store property; Capt. Ralph C. Manuel. Exchange Officer, and Lt. Robert C. Johnson, Civilian Personnel Officer to handle employee procurement.

In the meantime, plans for the activation of the station complement were being studied. Limited service recruits were being trained at Camp McCoy, Wis., for operational jobs at Camp Ellis, whose duties would include administration, providing food and clothing, housing, guarding, supervision of a health program for the troops in training, and scores of other functions necessary for

Main entrance to Camp Ellis.

efficient administration. A nucleus of experienced non-commissioned officers was selected from other installations within the service command for duty at Ellis.

On Feb. 27, 1943, General Order No. 3 activated Headquarters Company, with temporary station at Fort Sheridan, Ill. The Medical Company was activated Mar. 1 and the Military Police and Service Company Mar. 20.

The day Headquarters Company received its orders to move, it was sent to Fort Sheridan where it was attached to the reception center for quarters and rations. First Sgt. Michael Davidson, a colorful veteran whose military career began 56 years ago, was in charge of 64 enlisted men and they continued their basic training at Sheridan, preparing themselves for the special duties they would assume when the camp at Ellis opened.

Almost six weeks later, a motor convoy carrying 38 men left Sheridan for Ellis. The first truck of the convoy swung around the main gate in mid-afternoon on Apr. 12. At 6.30 p. m., three days later, Sgt. Davidson arrived by train with his contingent of men to complete the detachment of about 100 men. This advanced body included Headquarters, Medical and Military Police cadres, supplemented the Service Company troops that arrived on the 12th. Staff and cadre officers arrived on the 15th and the main body of Headquarters personnel a few days later.

Ellis looked like a gold rush town. The streets and sidewalks were one step from the barracks door, drainage was non-existant, and it became axiomatic that you could stand in the mud up to your knees with dirt blowing in your face. It was a wet spring, the clouds opening intermittently for 30 days.

Equipment and supplies were limited, thus organization problems, complicated by bad weather conditions, hampered the first activities.

Maj. Gen. Russell L. Maxwell, former chief of the United States North African Mission with headquarters in Cairo, Egypt, arrived on May 1, and became the camp commander. Among the most important changes in his staff organization was the appointment of Col. Spalding as Training Group commander and Col. Hans. C. Minuth to the post of Service Group director. Col. George E. Hartman, who for a few weeks was commanding officer of the Quartermaster Group, became a Brigadier General on May 14. The star was pinned on him by Gen. Maxwell and a few days later Gen. Hartman was named Inspector of the Army Service Forces Unit Training Center.

The Minute Man Flag.

Heavy rains refused to let up that first spring and although the swollen Spoon River which had overrun its banks in some of the training areas caused no major problems for the camp, the rains precipitated the worst flood conditions ever known in Central Illinois. Neighboring communities threatened by the surging flood waters of the Illinois River, sent appeals to Camp Ellis to help combat the impending devastation. Camp Ellis replied immediately by sending a detachment of men to the Beardstown area where they helped avert major disaster.

The official dedication of Camp Ellis took place on July 4. Some 50,000 visitors attended. The occasion was marked by considerable pomp and ceremony. Almost a month later, on August 1, Gen. Hartman was named Service Group commander. The next day the Prisoner of War Camp was activated. Though the Wacs did not arrive until the following January, their detachment, the 4624 Service Unit, was activated on August 16.

General staff duties called Gen. Maxwell to Washington and on Oct. 6 Gen. Hartman assumed command of Camp Ellis. Gen. Hartman, who was a great sports enthusiast, placed considerable emphasis on special service activities. The

Headquarters Officers found relaxation here.

Col. Sullivan presents Colors to civilian gua

General made some changes in organization but the mission of the camp was left unchanged during his short tenure of office, which ended on Dec. 18, when he was ordered to other duty preparatory to going overseas. Col. John S. Sullivan, who was Deputy Chief of Staff at Headquarters, Sixth Service Command, was ordered to Camp Ellis to take command.

Camp Ellis had its greatest period of growth and expansion in 1944, the war's most crucial year. The need for ASF units overseas was acute and Ellis turned them out speedily and efficiently. A number of changes were made in organization and in the assignment of key personnel. Most important staff changes were the appointment of Col. James F. Butler, former Service Command personnel officer as assistant to the commanding officer; Col. Wilbur C. Bechtold, former commanding officer of Fort Brady, Mich., as Executive Officer; Col. Raymond H. Bishop as Director of Training; Col. George T. Shank, formerly Commanding Officer at Fort Custer, Mich., as Director of Supply. Major departmental reorganization was the consolidation of military police, internal security and military intelligence under a single head, the Director of Security and Intelligence.

While training units for overseas service was the primary mission of Camp Ellis, energies were also devoted to many matters of less importance in accordance with War Department directives; for example, fat rendering programs, salvage of tin cans, waste paper and various types of scrap metals, all contributed to the nation's growing pool of resources for war. Control over

H & S Co. NCO Club.

Gen. Weible visits H & S Co. Non-Coms' Club.

fat issued saved the government over $11,000 in the six months period ending July, 1944. The camp's 200 acre "victory garden" saved $58,000 and helped ease the strain on the civilian market.

Camp Ellis made notable marks in every war fund drive. In four War Bond drives the camp rose from 20 to 100 per cent participation. After the Sixth drive more than 12 per cent of the civilian pay was going into war bonds each pay day. In 1944, Ellis took top honors in the service command for Infantile Paralysis drive and more than $8,000 was raised for the Red Cross.

The rivers rose again in April and Camp Ellis sent 5,000 troops to protect 300 miles of the Mississippi and Illinois Rivers in Southern Illinois. In June Quincy, Ill., was threatened by floods and Ellismen built and reinforced levees to save the power station which serviced many vital war plants.

The welfare of the enlisted man became one of the primary concerns of the administration. Bus service to neighboring towns was improved and free service to Galesburg was inaugurated in April, 1944. Sports was given a prominent place in off-duty curricula and competitions between units were sponsored by Special Services. In May, H & S Co. opened the camp's first Non-Commissioned Officers' Club. Other NCO clubs were opened shortly afterward.

The effectiveness of a commanding officer is reflected by the efficiency and coordination of the many headquarters functions under his jurisdiction. The Training Division, Post Engineer, Supply, Personnel, Fiscal, Security and Intelligence, Judge Advocate and the camp Adjutant Division, are the main cogs in the wheels which keep the camp running. These are discussed here. Other headquarters functions such as the Station Hospital and the various training groups are discussed in other chapters of this history.

The Training Division is responsible for the coordination of training, training facilities, training aids within the training groups, maintenance of status of training reports, and keeping higher headquarters informed of the current state of training. This includes inspection of units from date of activation or arrival here or until their departure on continental movement or to a Port of Embarkation.

In the decentralization of activities of the Training Division, sections were organized and given special missions and objectives. They were, namely: Control and Status of Training; Supply; Plans and Operations; Orientation and the Common Schools Section.

The latter section has trained and graduated thousands of Ellis soldiers in technical fields to which they were assigned here and in many cases over seas. The fields covered by the Common Schools section were administration and supply, bugler and messenger, crating and packing, weapons maintenance, chemical warfare, motor vehicle operators and mechanics, cooks and mess sergeants, and the demolition school.

Camp Ellis has some of the finest small arms ranges in the country. Consisting of 22 courses, the ranges are so

Col. Bishop braves Barber School.

H & S men ready for rapid fire.

The German Village.

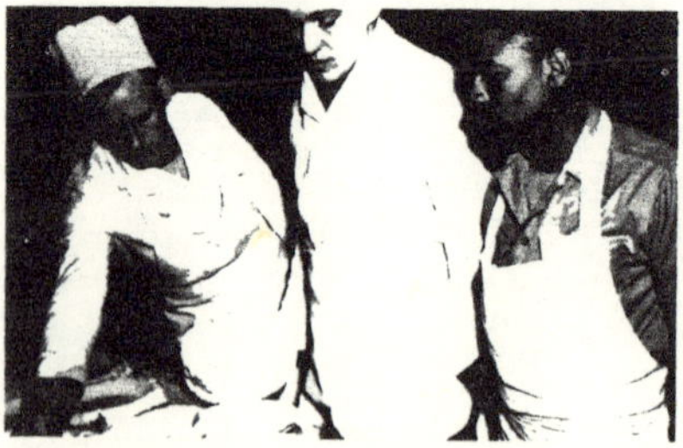

Students in Cooks and Bakers School.

constructed as to permit firing either simultaneously or independently into one danger area.

It is the responsibility of the Range sections to maintain and assign ranges, designate danger zones, and to close roads leading into danger zones. Besides the small arms ranges they also maintain four one thousand inch courses, a transition range which gives the rifleman practice in searching for targets; five squad-combat ranges; a close combat range; a 25 target pistol range and sub-machine gun course; an anti-aircraft range; two infiltration courses; a picturesque "German Village," which was designed primarily to teach the detection of land mines and booby traps; two bazooka and rifle grenade ranges and two live hand grenade courses.

The Post Engineer maintains the camp's buildings, roads and walks, water supply, electricity and heating, sewage disposal and new construction. Employing approximately 500 workers —all civilians—with five officers as supervisors, the Post Engineer performs every maintenance function of a large city government.

Among its employees are professional and skilled technicians who work in the heavy and light equipment shop, motor pool, sheet metal shop, carpenter shops, labor pool, plumbing shop, engineering, drafting, water supply, sewage, steam, electrical shop, personnel, property, and unskilled maintenance labor employed as janitors and laborers.

Maintenance Branch repairs 3000th vehicle.

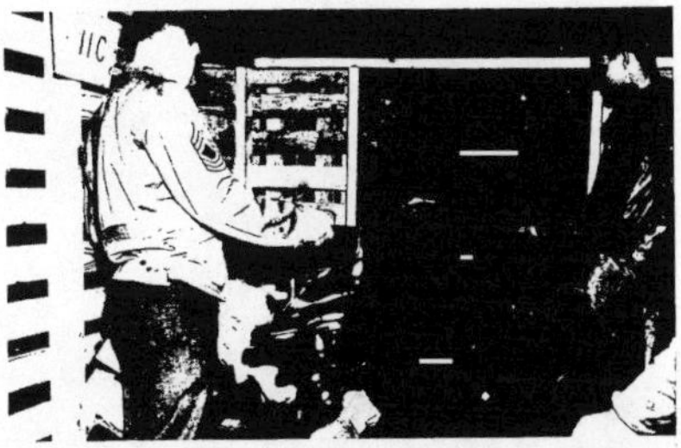

Supply Division issues clothing and equipment.

Taking off for the week end.

Sewage disposal plant.

Chapel No. 2. The war map in Headquarters PX.

Reports on operation of sewage plant were adopted for use as a national model by the Office of the Chief of Engineers in Washington. Another survey of design and operation was accepted as a model for the Sixth Service Command in September, 1944.

Primary function of the Supply Division is to service training and operating personnel. This division employs the largest number of workers of any division at Camp Ellis; more than 1,500 at its peak. This total included more than 400 prisoners of war.

Compared to a city, the Supply Division is the grocer, baker, parking lot, haberdasher, laundry, meat packer, gas company, coal dealer, telegraph office, shoe factory and a hundred other technical services—all wrapped into a huge combine to equip the soldier with what he needs to train and fight. In fact one of its biggest jobs was supplying the hundreds of overseas units that left Camp Ellis with complete equipment.

The Maintenance Branch, the largest in the Division, embraces the combined shops on the post and has the responsibility of repairing and reclaiming all property in the camp, plus quotas assigned in automotive repair by the Sixth Service Command. In 18 months, the sale of salvageable items netted Uncle Sam about $4,000 a month. Conversion of items to other uses saved another $4,500 a month, and the value of surplus material turned over to the Treasury Department for sale, further use, or lend-lease totaled $8,500 monthly.

The recruitment, selection and hiring of the personnel that helped build and maintain Camp Ellis was the responsibility of the Personnel Division. The development and expansion called for skilled workers, technicians and workers within the scarce categories. Then there was the constant need for replacement of military personnel transferred overseas by both civilians and physically disqualified soldiers. Also within the jurisdiction of this division is Special Services and the camp Chaplains. The Chaplains supervise the spiritual and moral welfare of the camp's military personnel. Services are conducted regularly for all religious faiths.

The protection and safety of camp personnel and property is the primary concern of the Security and Intelligence Division. From the day the camp opened, Ellis has had the best safety record in the Sixth Service Command. The Civilian Auxiliary police has grown with the camp and supplements the work of the regular MP's with a sizeable force.

Other headquarters Divisions, perhaps not as large in comparable size but equally as important, are the Fiscal and Judge Advocate Divisions and the office of the camp Adjutant.

The achievements of the four administrations may be measured by the grand jobs being accomplished by the Ellis-trained units in every theater of operation. The success of their efforts is also reflected in the following comments made by General Officers from higher headquarters after inspecting the camp.

MAJOR GENERAL HENRY S. AURAND, in his last visit to Camp Ellis, made only complimentary remarks on the work done in a talk to all officers of the camp. He thought that the non-commissioned officers of the Training Groups the finest he had seen anywhere. He commented on the interest and enthusiasm shown by the officers and enlisted personnel and likewise the civilians in their work.

BRIGADIER GENERAL BENJAMIN O.DAVIS of the I.G. Department, spent five days in the camp and on his departure stated there were no complaints of racial discrimination from any colored soldiers and that the colored soldiers here were more contented and better satisfied than at any camp he had visited. General Davis is the only Negro officer with the rank of General.

MAJOR GENERAL RUSSEL B. REYNOLDS, who relieved General Aurand as Service Commander in October, 1944, has repeatedly expressed his pleasure at the work done at Camp Ellis. After making an inspection of Camp Ellis, in December, 1944, he made the following statement: "It is obvious that everybody here is doing a good job. The zeal with which everybody undertakes his work is indeed stimulating".

MAJOR GENERAL WALTER L. WEIBLE, Director of Training Army Service Forces, on his three-day inspection trip in September, 1944, stated that we have as fine training aids as he has seen, anywhere; that the officers and men are enthusiastic, know their duties and work together as a well coordinated team; and that naturally he was immensely pleased.

Station Hospital

THE convoy of trucks slowly snaked its way through the roads of Camp Ellis. Huddled in the backs of the vehicles were 127 soldiers who gazed dubiously at the strange surroundings, the one-story barracks and the newly-constructed camp which now was their military home. These men, along with two officers were arriving in Camp Ellis as a cadre for the camp Station Hospital which was to grow into the largest institution of its kind in the Sixth Service Command. They were to be the pioneers in hospital work in this huge streamlined city which overnight came to life on the lush croplands of central Illinois. Theirs was the responsibility of laying the foundation for one of the largest Army hospitals in the command.

Much paper work had to be completed in Command Headquarters before the signal was sounded for the movement to Camp Ellis of the contingent of medical men. When the operating staff of the camp was organized in February, 1943, in Chicago's Civic Opera Building, Lt.-Colonel R. F. Olmsted was appointed camp surgeon. Immediately he began formulating plans for the operation of the Medical branch. During this uncertain period of organization the surgeon and his staff members acquainted themselves with the many problems of supply, equipment and personnel. They toured and inspected medical establishments at all posts in the Sixth Service Command. They made mental and paper notes. They observed keenly all operations. They studied carefully methods of solving intricate and complex problems. Before plans could be drawn up and submitted several trips to the site of Camp Ellis were necessary. These visits were made with the specific purposes of inspecting and checking the water supply and completing all preliminary planning.

After long hours of travels, inspections, planning and debating, the original plans for the medical facilities at Camp Ellis were ready. Partly, they had provided for one 1403-bed cantonment-type hospital, two dental clinics in the troop area, and one in the hospital area. Later, additions to the plans called for a 125-bed hospital compound for the care of prisoners of war.

The machinery for the operation of the Station Hospital had been assembled. It had been oiled, tested and primed. Its supervisor, Lt.-Colonel Herman Jacobson, had been selected. The element lacking was a capable personnel group to handle this delicate machinery. So on March 1, 1943, at Fort Sheridan, Illinois, the Medical Company, 1603 Service Unit, was activated. An advance "scouting" party was dispatched to Camp Ellis to establish a temporary dispensary and provide emergency hospital facilities in the troop area and to prepare for the arrival of the contingent of 127 men and two officers three days later. In a sense, members of this advance party were the real pioneers, as they were introduced to Camp Ellis on April 12. On April 17, the designation 1603 SU was changed to 1624 SU and, three days after this change, 426 enlisted men from the Limited Service School at Camp McCoy, Wisconsin, reported for duty with the Medical Company.

Thus everything was in readiness. Eleven medical officers, two medical administrative officers and a chief nurse and her assistant had reported for duty. Hospital headquarters were moved from Building 505 to the Station Hospital building. Hospital mess halls were opened. Property office, transportation system, receiving and evacuation office and an infirmary were established and on May 3 the first wards of the hospital were ready to receive patients.

Misfortune in the form of a fire then struck the expanding hospital. On May 5 the first permanent dispensary to be constructed and opened was par-

Bike riders reconditioning.

Reconditioning thru Archery.

tially destroyed by a blaze caused by a faulty heating system. All patients were immediately removed without loss of life or injury. Almost two weeks later another disaster struck, this time outside of camp but nevertheless necessitating assistance from the medical corps. Heavy rains caused the Illinois river to overflow and wild waters flooded the countryside around Beardstown and other communities near Camp Ellis. Officers and enlisted men were dispatched at once to the flood scenes and executed their duties so admirably that praise from all sources, civilian and military, was never-ending. No sooner had the weary medics returned than Mother Nature staged another act. A freak and violent windstorm swept over Camp Ellis and completely destroyed a long corridor—Kirk Corridor—in the hospital area. The Medical Company responded promptly and cleared away the debris. No person was injured.

It was a rough initiation for the newly-arrived medics, but they weathered all the storms like seasoned veterans.

Throughout the months of May and June the hospital continued to grow. X-ray, out patient, clinic and hospital facilities were established and expanded. On the first of June, 420 beds were set up. A modern dental clinic with 10 operating chairs was in operation. The pharmacy was opened June 5 and three days later the Orthopedic clinic was ready to receive patients. On order of the camp surgeon an Emergency Medical Unit (Mobile) was activated on June 10. The end of June saw 15 wards handling soldier-patients.

Orthopedic Shoe Shop.

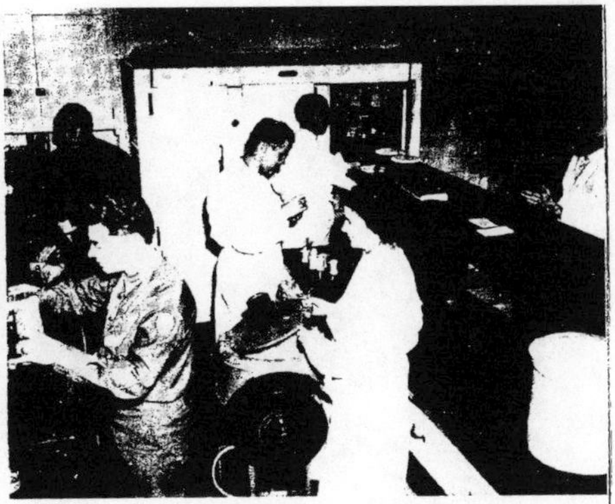

A well-equipped laboratory.

The Station Hospital with its facilities was one of the chief points of interest to hundreds during the dedication day celebration on July 4, 1943. Civilians were astounded when told that the Hospital occupied 140 acres; that one of the corridors was 2,939 feet long; that it had the latest X-ray, surgical and diagnostic equipment available. They looked pop-eyed at this sprawling military medical institution built in a series of units in the western part of the encampment.

Colonel Olmsted was relieved of his post as camp surgeon in August, 1943, and was succeeded by the Station Hospital commander, Col. Jacobson, who maintained this post until November, 1943, when Colonel H. C. Johannes was appointed camp surgeon. Col. Jacobson, now a full colonel, again took over

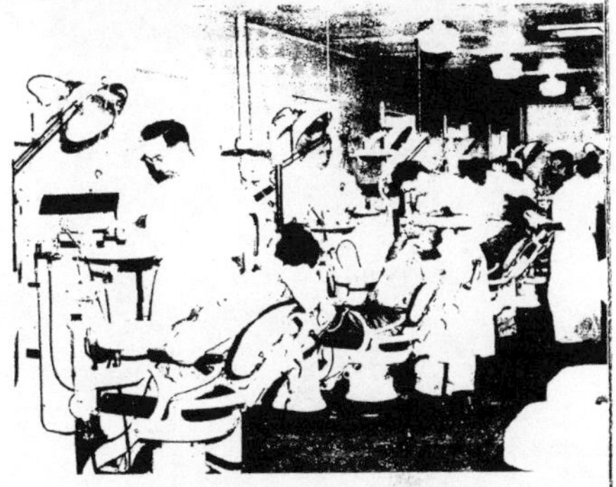

One of the modern Dental Clinics.

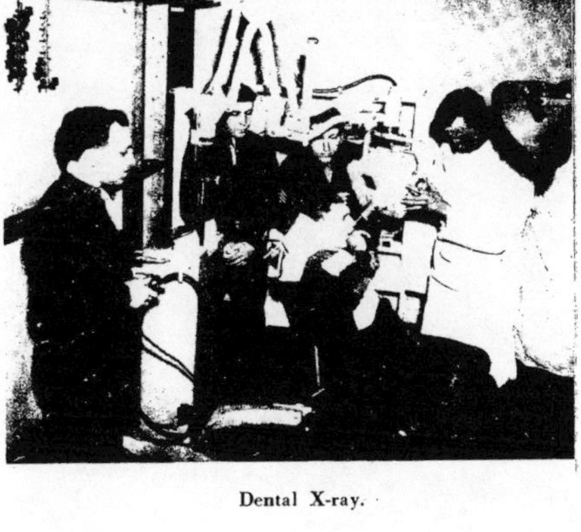

Dental X-ray.

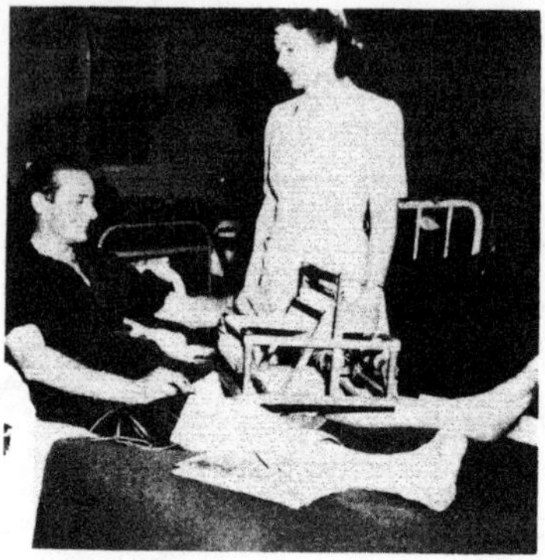

A patient tries weaving.

the camp surgeon's post after Col. Johannes left. The consolidation of camp surgeon and camp Hospital Commander into one office saved personnel and operated more efficiently. Colonel Olmsted is now serving in India.

Through the fall and winter of Camp Ellis' first year and through the early months of 1944, the Station Hospital continued to expand. More facilities were added to better care for GI Joe. No expense was spared in obtaining the most modern equipment the medical world could provide. Spare time of the patients was utilized with the help of the cheerful Gray Ladies of the Red Cross who worked tirelessly toward the erection of a cozy, home-like Red Cross house in the hospital area. WACs made their appearance on the hospital scene in January of 1944, and were assigned as clerks and technicians in the various departments. On March 24, a chapel was completed for hospital personnel and patients.

The Ellis Station Hospital made news in papers from coast to coast, in August, 1944, when Captain I. J. Spiegel, neurosurgeon from Shick General Hospital, Clinton, Iowa, was flown to the camp to enable him to perform a delicate brain operation.

Hospital routine here was as prosaic as that of any other station hospital. But the addition of the Re-conditioning Section immediately injected doses of novelty into the entire training program. One of the most interesting and extensive phases of training on the Station Hospital roster, the Re-conditioning program was intended to eliminate the boredom that is usually associated with hospitalization. Its aim was to help patients reach their physical peak before they are returned to duty, or, if necessary, to civilian life. Col. Jacobson, hospital commander, inaugurated the program in March, 1944, and it was a constantly expanding activity. Lt. Stansbury was made director of the program in August, 1944, and developed such hobbies, diversions and games as repair work and mechanics, weaving, ornamental baskets, archery, building of furniture pieces, hand wrestling, repair of automobiles, radios, exercises, and table tennis.

The Rabbit hunt.

Beagle hounds added a unique twist to the entire re-conditioning program. Introduction of rabbit hunts for the patients, many of them Purple Heart vets from Anzio, Cassino, France, and the Pacific, was a great step forward. They used six beagle hounds to round up the cotton-tails which scampered around the hospital area. The only patients given authority to participate in the hunts were those whose status was described as "almost well." The patients carried no other ammunition but stones and sticks. It should be stated unequivocally that, despite the sniffing, snooping beagle hounds who picked up scents with every sniff, the patients seldom if ever managed to snare a speedy bobtail. But what the patients did derive from three hours of rabbit-hunting was an afternoon of wholesome, clean fun, much-needed exercise, fresh air, and plenty of sunshine.

The Station Hospital slowly but surely was transformed from an awkward looking building squatting in the mud and weeds to a dressed-up structure surrounded by flowers, shrubbery and trim-cut grass.

Thousands of patients have walked the long corridors of the hospital, tired, sick, lonely. These same individuals left the hospital full of spirit, ambitious and with the glow of good health—this to the credit of hospital personnel. Nothing was left undone if it was to benefit the American soldier.

Prisoners of War

THE confinement of German prisoners of war was an important function assigned to Camp Ellis, in addition to its primary mission of serving as a large unit training center. But wartime secrecy shrouded plans for the PW's. Visitors at the dedication ceremonies noted the high, barbed wire fences enclosing one section of the camp; they observed that there were approximately 60 barracks in the enclosure, and they knew that the guards' watchtowers and the big, mounted searchlights meant that this area was prepared to hold PW's. Some predicted Japs would be brought in—others, that Germans were due to arrive soon—and still others held that the stockade would never be put to use. The Army made no effort to settle the issue or to satisfy civilian curiosity.

The first official announcement concerning the PW's came at the end of August, when the Public Relations Office released a statement that more than a thousand Germans had been transferred to Ellis. They had reached this camp under escort guard of 29 August 1943.

The PW camp had been activated on 21 August. It was originally designated as the Camp Ellis Interment Camp, but on 31 August its name was changed to the Camp Ellis, Illinois, Prisoner of War Camp. The 475th and the 476th Military Police Escort Guard Companies were assigned to this camp for guard duty, and the Headquarters and Headquarters Detachment was set up to handle administrative duties and personnel matters.

On 8 September 1943 Colonel Hans C. Minuth, Cavalry, was assigned as the Commanding Officer of the PW camp, which then had a total strength of 308 American enlisted men and officers and 2,672 PW's.

Col. Minuth had served with General Maxwell on the Intelligence staff of the Army of Occupation in Germany; he was a linguist of ability and had devoted long study to the customs and background of the German people.

To eliminate any excess overhead personnel, the two Military Police Escort Guard companies, the 349th and the 683rd, were consolidated with the Headquarters Detachment on 16 April 1944 to form the Headquarters and Headquarters Guard Company, with Captain Robert O. Bishop, C.M.P., detailed as the commanding officer.

On 13 August 1944, Lt. Colonel C. P. Evers, Inf., assumed command on the departure of Col. Minuth. Early in December he was promoted to full colonel. Colonel Evers was one of the "pioneer"officers who helped Camp Ellis through its early trials. He was in the training division until June, 1943, when he went to the Command and General Staff school at Ft. Leavenworth, Kansas, after which he assumed command of four Army Specialized Training Program schools in Chicago. He returned to Ellis in May, 1944.

107 PW's of Polish extraction who had been interviewed and carefully screened by representatives of the Free Polish Government were shipped to Ft. Wadsworth, N. Y. for eventual transfer to England. There they were to be trained with the Polish Forces in that country.

Only four deaths among the PW's have occurred since they were first received at Ellis. Three of these took place at the camp and one at Percy Jones Hospital. All were buried with full military honors as prescribed by the Geneva Convention.

In order to separate Austrians and Anti-Nazis from the Nazis and thereby reduce the number of guards required and also, to attain maximum work from the PW's, a new stockade some distance from the old one was set up by simply

enclosing a selected area with a wire fence. No guards are necessary with these PW's who carry a card stating that they go about the camp without guards during work hours. Approximately 330 PW's were in the separate compound.

Conditions at the Ellis PW camp have always been in strict accord with the provisions of the Geneva Convention. It has also been the policy of the camp to provide the captives with ample physical and mental activity to keep them busy and healthy. Washington authorities have stated this is one of the best PW camps in the country.

The PW's received the same rations that are specified for all American soldiers in the Sixth Service Command. But they did not get ice cream or "cokes" or candy when there was a scarcity of such commodities for the American army; the only ice cream they got during that period was as prescribed in their regular rations, usually once a week. In the enclosure a Post Exchange was operated for their benefit. The profit went into a fund which was drawn on from time to time to pay for the occasional "extras" in refreshments, rations or recreational activity.

Non-commissioned PW officers were not forced to work, except in a supervisory capacity. They may work if they desire. Geneva Conference rules

are definite on this point. The PW's received an allowance of 10c per day, and they got 80c a day whenever they were detailed on Class 2 labor (all labor other than Class 1, which is that done in connection with the maintenance of the entire PW camp). No pay was received for Class 1 labor. The working day was limited to a maximum of 12 hours, including travel time to and from work. Prisoners worked six days a week, inasmuch as the Geneva Conference provides that one day a week shall be theirs for rest.

A large field for sports and recreation was located at one end of the stockade, and the men themselves organized teams and indulged in games, soccor being their favorite sport. Movies were shown to PW's, who paid for admission. Prisoners received a monthly physical inspection. Regular religious services were conducted by both Protestant and Catholic chaplains. One of the prisoners was an ordained Catholic priest and said mass on frequent occasions. Others belonged to Protestant faiths, and some to what is known as the 'Free Church.'

The German soldier has always been taught to respect rank and authority, and it was noted that this held true among the PW's. They were allowed to select their own spokesman who would serve as a liaison between them and

American authorities. Ordinarily a German noncom would have been chosen, but at Ellis the PW's agreed to be represented by a "soldat" (private of about 35) who had been a corporation lawyer in Germany.

The prisoners were permitted to send and receive censored mail but were limited to the sending of one letter and one card a week. Visitors could be received only upon authorization by the camp commander, with approval by the Provost Marshal General of the Army.

The PW's were used successfully in many types of work in the camp area and in nearby communities. "Side camps" were in operation near several canneries. On 3 May 1944 the first of these branch camps was established at canneries. Other types of work done by the PW's included labor in the camp's victory gardens, the lumber yards, the clothing warehouses and other buildings in the warehouse area (doing loading, unloading, repairing clothing, shoes, etc.), work in the Post Engineer Motor Pool (repairing automobile engines and machinery), cutting grass, digging ditches, clean-up duties in the service clubs, K. P. duty at both officers' mess and Headquarters mess for enlisted men, and work on the railroad tracks running into the camp. They also worked in the Post Engineers Section, operating mimeograph machines and doing odd jobs.

The only German officers in the PW camp at Ellis were six medical officers who were brought in to undertake medical treatment and care of PW's under the supervision of an American medical officer, both in the stockade dispensary and in the PW's three wards at the Camp Ellis station hospital. One of these three wards was devoted to malaria patients, one to surgical treatment and one to general medical treatment. The wards were located at the far east end of the hospital and were enclosed by barbed wire.

Training

OVERSEAS training was assigned to five major groups under the direction of the camp's training division. The bulk of the unit training mission was accomplished by three groups, the Quartermaster, Engineer and Medical. The Signal Group merely trained a few units and was later transferred to another camp. In early 1944, the Training Group was activated to train individual soldiers before they were assigned to their respective units.

When Camp Ellis completed its mission as a unit training center, it could point with pride to the 456 units trained here, ranging from huge engineer regiments to small medical detachments of less than a dozen men. Of this total, the camp trained 58 different types of units.

Quartermaster Group

THE time was late 1942. War Department officials had just completed discussions and conferences relative to organizing a Quartermaster Corps unit training center. From southern Wyoming they summoned Colonel George E. Hartman, veteran of 27 years of Army service, who was serving as executive officer of the Quartermaster Replacement Training Center of Fort Warren. Colonel Hartman had not been in Washington long when he found himself seated at a long conference table around which were gathered prominent Army chieftains. They told him of their plans for the organization of a QM training center and then informed him that his was the job of forming the first unit training center ever to be operated by the Quartermaster Corps.

Back across the country sped Colonel Hartman. His final stop was Vancouver Barracks in the southwestern part of the state of Washington. It was here, then, on January 1, 1943, that the first Quartermaster Unit Training Center was activated under his supervision. Plans called for the entire installation to move to Camp Ellis which at that time was under construction.

Activation day found a large contingent of commissioned and enlisted personnel handpicked for the important task of operating the training center machinery. The officers were selected from Quartermaster posts at Camp Lee, Virginia, and Fort Warren, Wyoming, and were chosen because of their excellent background and experience.

Camp Ellis was announced as ready for occupancy in March and Colonel Hartman, accompanied by Colonel A. N. Stubblebine, Jr., and Lt. Colonel Glenn J. Jacoby, was called to a conference at Sixth Service Command Headquarters. Plans for the first Army Service Forces Unit Training Center were discussed. Colonel Hartman was instructed to return immediately to Vancouver Barracks to select qualified officers and enlisted personnel for the Quartermaster Branch of the new center. The initial allotment of personnel consisted of 41 officers and 116 enlisted men for instructor personnel and trainer overhead.

It was on April 26, 1943, that the first contingent from the Washington installation rolled into Camp Ellis. Fourteen days later the second group of officers and enlisted men, who came from Vancouver, arrived at the Illinois camp. This allotment of personnel was later increased because certain functions were assumed by the Quartermaster Group Headquarters which had not been contemplated in the original assignment. The Motor Training Branch had been originally established as a part of camp headquarters, but officials later decided to transfer to the Quartermaster Group the operation of all the motor training schools.

Upon opening of Camp Ellis, the QM Group was designated as the QM Branch. Colonel Hartman, with his years of Army background and study and his activity in the organization of the Group since its natal day, was considered the logical man to head the new organization. He was placed in command, with Lt. Colonel Jacoby as Executive Officer. The group had been in operation only a few weeks when word was received that Colonel Hartman had been promoted to the rank of Brigadier General. General Hartman was immediately assigned as second in command of Camp Ellis while Lt. Colonel Jacoby assumed command of the Quartermaster Group, 1634 Service Unit, now redesignated from Quartermaster Branch under authority of General Order No. 14, Headquarters, Army Service Forces Unit Training Center, Camp Ellis, Illinois, dated 31 May 1943.

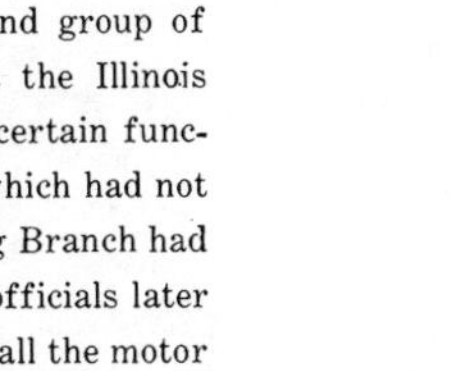

Repairing Tire Tube

Engine Maintenance

Lt. Colonel Jacoby retained the command of the QM Group from 1 June 1943 until 11 July 1944, at which time Lt. Colonel Jackson R. Webb assumed command. Special duty in the European and Mediterranean theaters from mid-January 1944 through mid-April of the same year called Colonel Jacoby from his post at Camp Ellis, and during his absence Lt. Colonel George Martin assumed his duties. During the time that Colonel Martin was in Command of the Group Lt. Colonel Webb was Executive Officer. Upon the return of Lt. Colonel Jacoby, Lt. Colonel Webb resumed his former duties as Director of Training. Lt. Colonel Jacoby received orders transferring him to an overseas assignment in July, and Lt. Colonel Webb again assumed command. He retained the position from 12 July 1944 to 4 October 1944 at which time he was assigned duties as Director of Supply Division, Camp Ellis, Illinois. Major Louis J. Krakoff, who had been Director of Control and Status of Training, assumed command.

The Quartermaster Group was confronted with problems, as any newly formed group might be. Difficulties arose in handling and housing an influx of personnel. To meet the immediate need of further accommodations, it became necessary to quarter the 309th Battalion, numbering 648 enlisted men, in tents in the Quartermaster area. The situation was soon alleviated as adequate accommodations became available.

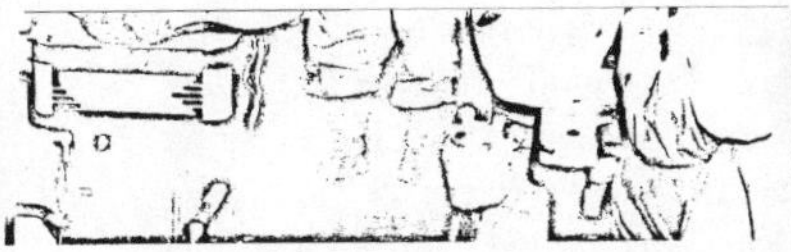

Mobile Shoe Repair Shop

Mobile Tailor Shop

A Mobile Laundry Unit

Baking Bread in the Field

At the same time, it was found necessary to transfer the 539th, 548th, and 553rd Quartermaster Service Battalions with very little personnel to other stations. These battalions later returned to Camp Ellis for completion of their training.

Perhaps the greatest problem of all was in the assignment of men. Many were limited service personnel sent to Camp Ellis from Fort Sheridan during the summer of 1943. Group commanders discussed with Medical Officers the suitability of these men for overseas duty. Our officers struggled with proper placement of these men and found discouraging moments, but only those suitable for Quartermaster duties remained. Men not physically qualified for overseas duty were no longer sent to the Group.

Obstacle Course

The GI assigned to Camp Ellis' Quartermaster Group was given a vigorous training program. This program was the first venture of the Quartermaster Corps into real unit training and consequently it was something new to all concerned—including the GI. The War Department had found that it would be advantageous to form a unit whose personnel would remain together from the first day of activation. Of all the lessons learned at the first Quartermaster Unit Training Center, Vancouver Barracks, the most important had been that responsibility for unit training must lie within the unit itself. The first QM group at Ellis pioneered. Methods had to be learned by trial and error. Much of the credit for the basic theory and the actually proven proceedures in use today must be given to "those early sons" of Camp Ellis.

Notwithstanding the fact that the basic principle of unit training was the training within the unit by the unit officers and non-commissioned officers themselves, it was necessary that certain common schools for the training of specialists be established. The camp headquarters, therefore, created schools which performed a creditable job in training certain technicians.

Other schools for certain specialists, whose training was not provided for in the camp common schools or within the unit themselves, were created by the Quartermaster Group.

The Spring of 1944 found the first Quartermaster units ready for overseas assignment. Almost every type of Quartermaster unit in the Army today had been trained, including laundry, bakery, fumigation and bath, salvage collection, salvage repair, refrigeration, truck companies, sales companies, service companies and QM battalion headquarters.

Units were trained under the program known as Mobilization Training

Program 10—1 which included a thirteen week program of training broken down into four weeks of basic training, four weeks of technical training, four weeks of tactical training, and one week of review and inspections.

Bayonet Practice

It was "up early and to bed early" for soldiers of the Group. There was plenty to do. In thirteen weeks green "civilians" in uniform were schooled and drilled, taught to fire the .30 caliber rifle, the rocket launcher, the rifle grenade, and the .30 and .50 caliber machine guns, with the efficiency of an old timer. They went through bayonet assault courses in mud and rain and crawled on their stomachs thru infiltration courses. Basic training was rough, but every soldier was given as much knowledge of his weapons and as much proficiency in their use as time allotted to insure, as far as humanly possible, his ability to protect himself.

The fact that the Quartermaster units performed a technical supply job did not mean that there would not come a day when they would be pulled into line to fight side by side with infantry, artillery or other combat forces.

The troops were drilled and trained to fight along with the Infantry, if necessary, and attended schools where they learned all of the tricks of the trade of the Quartermaster soldier. Some became bakers, while others were assigned to the Quartermaster Sales Company, the Salvage Section of Reclamation Section, and other units.

Definite efforts were made in the early days of the QM Group to do away with the sharp line of demarcation between Basic Military and Technical Training, since experience had proved that there was an apparent let-down among the men when Basic Military Training was terminated and Technical Training began. Therefore, to retain the interest of the soldier, this difficulty was overcome by beginning Technical Training during the third, fourth,

Handling High Explosives at Iowa Ordnance Depot.

fifth and sixth weeks of Basic Training, and extending some of the Basic work which might ordinarily have ceased at the end of the sixth week.

Functions of the Training Division were exercised through several branches and sections, including the Basic Military Branch, Technical Training Branch, Motor Training Branch and Training Aids Branch. These branches in turn were divided into various sections, while in the headquarters of the Training Division itself there were several sections, including operations, coordination and orientation.

The Basic Military Branch was responsible for the preparation of training programs, training memoranda, training guides and for the interpretation of War Department directives on basic military training. The instruction and supervision of all technical training of all Quartermaster units was supervised by the Technical Training Branch. Since there are many different kinds of Quartermaster companies, there were many different types of technical training to be given, and the Technical Training Branch was accordingly divided into several sections, each dealing with a particular type of training.

Training of men to become bakers, to work in Fummigation and Bath Companies, in the Laundry, Refrigeration Companies, Salvage Section, Reclamation Section, QM Service Companies, Quartermaster Sales Company, Graves Registration and Motor Branch progressed more than satisfactorily from the first organization of the Group.

Versatility in training marked the Quartermaster Service Companies training program. Men of the 27 Service Companies of the QM Group had to prove their mettle before being approved as qualified service troops by putting to practical use, in April, 1944, at one of four mid-western plants, the theoretical knowledge learned at Camp Ellis. The training "depot training," was practiced at the Granite City Engineer Depot, the Sangamon Ordnance Depot, Iowa Ordnance Depot and the Elwood Arsenal.

While at these plants the Service Companies were given practical training in loading and unloading railroad cars, warehousing, sorting and identification of ordnance material and ammunition, operating materials, handling equipment, sorting and classifying general supplies, packing and crating and many other functions peculiar to the particular plant . . . the work involved skill and great care.

At the Ordnance plant, work consisted of loading and unloading explosives and men in one particular area were taught to handle TNT. This depot training was incorporated into the unit schedule whenever possible, after fundamental technical subject had been completed.

Troops were given practical experience in loading and blocking vehicles at the Quartermaster Service Company's "Short Line" constructed north of Q Street, Camp Ellis, in the early Spring of 1944. The novel training equipment consisted of a dummy box car and a dummy flat car where QM troops were taught how to load and block vehicles of all types from jeep to 10-ton trailer, according to Army specification.

A new program in vehicle recovery was inaugurated in April, 1944, by the Quartermaster Technical Training Branch for all Salvage Collecting Companies. The program as set up prepared trainees for any problem that would be encountered later in a theater of operations.

Soldiers learned to recover vehicles under blackout conditions. Dummy

Salvage Work with Oxy-acetelene Torch

Fighting the Spring Flood of 1944

Building a Sand Bag Levee

Bathing in the Field

vehicles were found to be impractical and in order to provide actual machines —jeeps, two and one half ton trucks, scout cars, tank turrets and tank bodies were brought from Chicago to Ellis. It was hard work "rescuing" these old crates in pitch-black night. The men located their "quarry" by compass and map.

The Illinois river again on a rampage in April, 1944, provided an outlet for experience accumulated by the Quartermasters during the thirteen week program. There was no glory to be handed out to the Quartermasters for the part they played in holding the river at Waterloo, Ill., within its banks. It was mud and water and sand bags and long nights without sleep. They worked hand-in-hand with the Engineers.

Camp Ellis had been alerted for flood duty on Monday, April 20. Early that morning 500 men from the 1309 Engr. Construction Battalion were ordered to the scene. Eight hours later the Quartermasters were called.

A "tent city" was set up on the school grounds of the local high school. The job was Herculean. Working on 12-hour shifts, the back-breaking labor consisted of filling sand bags and transporting them either by hand or by truck to the levees. Snow fences were erected to form a brace for the sand bags. Soldiers equipped with hip-boots periodically checked the sides of the levees.

In September, 1944, a plan was put into effect for the gradual closing of the Quartermaster Group. A large number of Quartermaster units had departed from Camp Ellis and only six Quartermaster Service Companies required further training before they would be ready for overseas duty.

Steps were taken to reduce the number of officers and enlisted personnel and to eliminate many functions. All of the remaining companies were consolidated into one area, and the Quartermaster Group Headquarters itself operated more or less as a provisional battalion headquarters with a strength of seven officers and 16 enlisted men.

Many of the officers and enlisted personnel in the Quartermaster Group Headquarters had been together since the start of the Quartermaster Unit Training Center at Vancouver Barracks, Washington. These men exhibited initiative, patience and co-operation in creating the first Quartermaster Group at Camp Ellis. Their job had not been easy.

On the fifteenth of September, 1944, the Officers' Mess of the Quartermaster Group was closed. A few officers remained to complete archives for each unit and to dispose of unnecessary files as well as to prepare other records for permanent storage.

The significance of the accomplishments of the Quartermaster Group is crystallized in the letter of commendation, dated 9 January 1945, from Col. Joseph P. Aleshire, Inspector General of the Sixth Service Command, quoted below:

> "Records indicate that one hundred twenty-four (124) Quartermaster Corps Units were trained at Camp Ellis, Illinois, during the period 26 April 1943 to 15 December 1944, on which date the Quartermaster Group was deactivated. POM inspection made by the office of the Service Command Inspector General, Sixth Service Command, of these units indicated commendable work on the part of Quartermaster Group personnel of the Training Center in supervising the organizing, training and administrative records of such units. To my knowledge, not a single Quartermaster Unit, trained at Camp Ellis, Illinois, was rejected at the port or held back for further training."

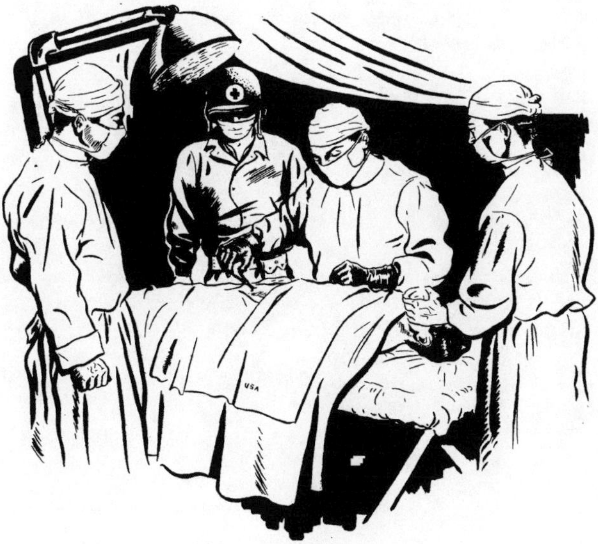
USA

Medical Group

THE story of the heroic work of the Medical Corps in World War II is known to millions. But known to only a handful is that many of these soldiers, who have been distinguishing themselves on the battlefield or performing their duty under adverse conditions in the rear areas, were trained at Camp Ellis. It's a glowing tribute to Camp Ellis and to its Medical Group that its Training Center, called the largest such unit in the Army, and organized in early 1943, trained almost every type of medical unit in operation, from the 11-man Malaria Control and Survey Units to the 1,000-bed General Hospitals and Medical Battalions and sent men to battlefronts all over the world.

Although May 6 marked the arrival at Camp Ellis of the first officers and enlisted men for the Medical Unit Training Center, official records state that the Medical Group, designated as the 1644th Service Unit, was activated June 1, 1943, per General Orders No. 14, Headquarters ASFUTC, Camp Ellis, from the 1644th Medical Branch which was activated April 19, 1943, and inactivated by the above general order.

Colonel Roland N. Holcombe was placed in command of the Medical Branch and took over his duties on April 28, 1943. He came from Washington, D. C., where he was an executive officer in the training division of the Army Service Forces. His military career dates back to November, 1917, when he received a First Lieutenant's commission and was immediately ordered to active service, reporting to the Medical Officer's Training Camp, then located at Fort Riley, Kansas. Upon completion of his training, he was ordered to a division at Ft. Lewis, Washington. Then Col. Holcombe organized a special medical unit and went overseas with it in June, 1918. Upon his return to the States, he was discharged at Camp Lee, Va. In 1923, he entered the Reserve Corps and was ordered to active duty in September, 1940, as a Major. He was made a Lieutenant Colonel in April, 1941, and promoted to Colonel in May, 1943.

Headquarters Company, 1644th S. U., was activated originally as Headquarters Medical-Signal Co., but growing functions of Headquarters Company made necessary a separate administration and supervision. The 1644th S. U. organized and coordinated the training of a great variety of medical units ranging in size from general hospitals to malaria control units. The mission of the Unit was . . . "to train and ready units to take the field and perform efficiently their duties in servicing combat troops." How well this mission has been accomplished is attested to by the large number of men and medical units which have left Camp Ellis ready to perform their duties on the fighting fronts in a manner designed to uphold the high standards of the Army Medical Corps.

To achieve this high standard of efficiency and speed with a minimum of overhead personnel, 1644th S. U. Medical Group made plans which:

1. Stressed the necessity of training the greatest number of medical department technicians in the shortest possible time.

2. Took advantage of the efficiency in training made possible by central control of units, uniform instruction, close supervision and fullest possible use of available equipment afforded by the Unit Training Center system.

Caring for patients on Hospital Train.

Hospital Train Kitchen.

3. Enabled units to function as a whole during their unit and advanced training phases.

This form of organization was designed to give men training equivalent to that in the regular enlisted technicians school, and, at the same time, to give all individuals of units technical training in their respective specialties, thus performing the additional purpose of moulding them into a cohesive unit.

The inadvisability of unit commanders attempting to train so many different specialists and medical technicians, the shortage of medical officers in the units, the varying degrees of technical training of incoming enlisted men and the need for refresher and advanced courses teaching the latest techniques and procedures, made evident the need for Medical Training Schools in the training of units under the jurisdiction of the 1644th S. U.

So vitally important in the highly-geared program were these schools that merely to mention them or pass over their function too lightly would be a grave injustice to the men responsible for their organization and to the men who reaped the benefits of their programs. These training schools were the hub around which the entire Medical Group training revolved.

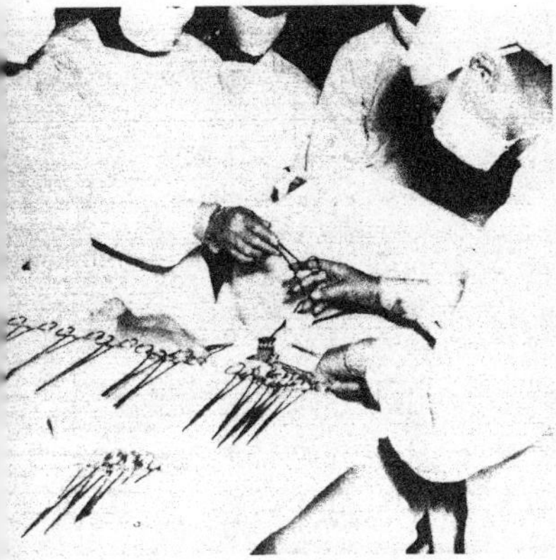

An operation in the field.

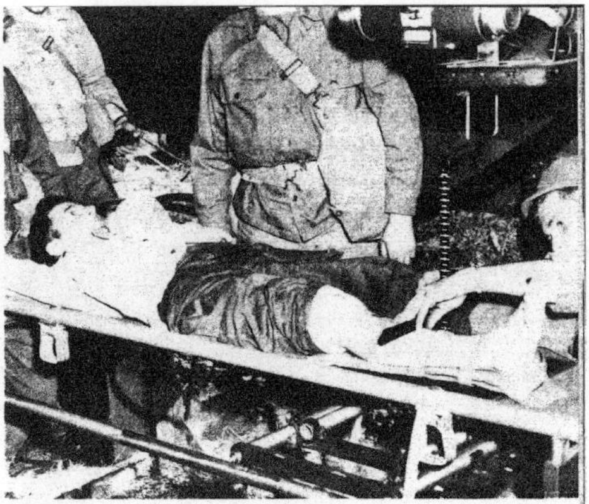

X-ray Students at work.

The first school to be opened was the Medical Administrative School which did not take over the training of basic clerks but instead concentrated on those clerks who already had completed the basic course, those men who had sufficient experience in Army administration and men with the required civilian experience to warrant attendance. The school was necessary for two principal reasons. First, there was a noticeable shortage of skilled clerks with a knowledge of specialized medical forms and procedures; second, there was the need for uniformity in administrative procedures among all the medical units.

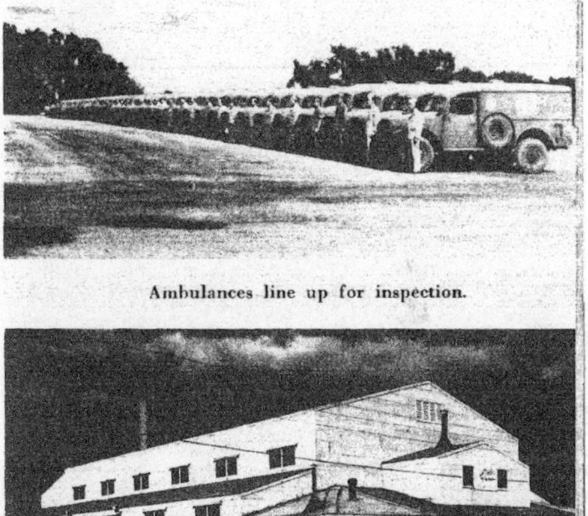

Ambulances line up for inspection.

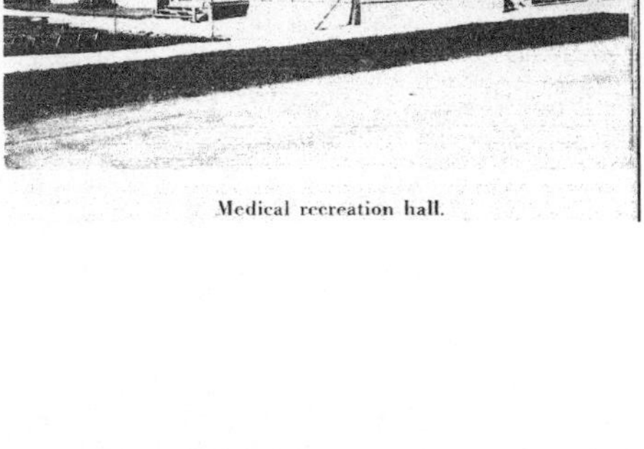

Medical recreation hall.

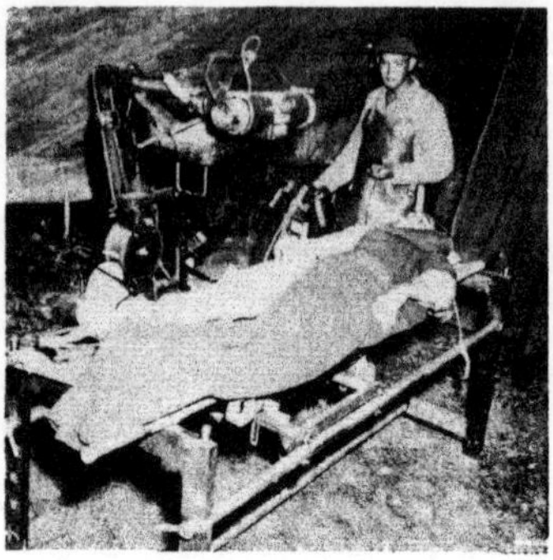

A Mobile X-Ray.

One of the most important schools to be set up was the Pharmacy Technician School, instituted in May, 1943, the sole purpose of which was to qualify men not previously experienced in pharmacy. After graduation these men were qualified to work in the Army Hospital Pharmacy performing such duties as keeping records, filling prescriptions, galencial pharmacy and related tasks. The first class began its studies early in June of 1943. Classes ran until September when notification was received to prepare for an enrollment of an advance class of pharmacy technicians, the first class of which enrolled during the last week in September and continued for four weeks. Later the school took on the added function of a central manufacturing laboratory serving three dispensaries.

The X-ray Technicians School was organized in May, 1943, with the primary mission to train basic students in the use of field equipment under field conditions. To obtain additional instructors a thorough and rigid examination was given to all men with previous X-ray experience. Although all the men had some knowledge of the subject, the majority of them failed to pass. This showed the necessity for advanced training. Two schedules then were devised. One was drawn up for the basics which condensed the usual three-month training period into two months and the other, for advanced students, was four weeks long. On June 28, 1943, the basic class with 10 students and the advanced class with 14 students began their studies. The greater part of the work was accomplished in the field and combat conditions were simulated as much as possible. At the end of the eighth advanced class, the school ceased operation. Because of the vital need for quick, efficient X-raying of patients throughout the camp, the school made arrangements to take over the making of X-rays. After two months as a clinic, the school was re-opened and courses resumed.

The organization of the Dental Technician School posed a problem not present in the creation of the other schools. Instead of organizing a course of study for the development of one type of technician, the Dental School had to be prepared to graduate two kinds of technicians, namely, a dental technician and a dental assistant. Although different courses were prepared, each closely adhered to one central theme of instruction -emphasis on improvisation and simulation of field conditions, even to the extent of having students make their own tools, instruments and other mechanical apparatus. A nine-week program was put into effect for the training of dental assistants and a three-month course for schooling of dental laboratory technicians. The dental technician course was a balanced training program prepared so that the graduate would be able to take the field on short notice as an integral part of a numbered hospital or specialized unit, while the main object of the dental assistants course was to create the understanding that a well-trained dental assistant could contribute to the efficiency by at least one-third of all military personnel through an increase in the amount of dental service rendered.

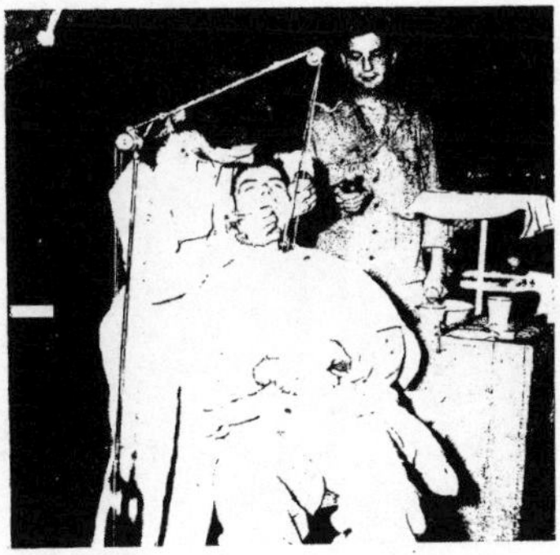

Dental treatment in the field.

The Laboratory Technicians School was established to qualify basic students as medical laboratory technicians and also to give those men already classified as such an opportunity to become more proficient in the laboratory and better acquainted with the latest techniques and procedures. The school operated two separate courses in laboratory technology, one for graduates of enlisted technicians school and one for basic students. The basic course ran for nine weeks, while the advanced course was four weeks long.

The Medical Technicians School was organized June 28, 1943. The course was of four weeks duration, after which the men were assigned to work in hospital wards for another four weeks. On the completion of the eight-week course they were recommended to their units as being eligible for rating as med-

Litter bearers work under assimilated fire.

ical technicians. Five classes were carried through to completion before the school ceased active training in November of the same year. A total of 550 men completed the training.

The Surgical Technicians School was started in May 1943. Intended to qualify men for work in an Army hospital, the school drew its personnel from the ranks of the inexperienced. The school was in operation a little more than five months and graduated 760 students. In addition to those authorized to attend the school from the units in training, other men were accepted from the Medical detachments of a Signal Corps unit and from an Engineering unit. The type of instruction consisted of formal lectures, conferences, demonstrations, practical applicatory exercises and examinations.

The inexperience of the personnel assigned to the first medical units activated at Camp Ellis made the necessity for training men as sanitary technicians as clear as the proverbial crystal. Very few had any knowledge of the subject and trained men were not available from other Army schools. With this need recognized, Medical Group Headquarters organized the Sanitary Technicians School and the first nine-week schedule started in June, 1943. Because classrooms were not available classes were held outdoors during the first few weeks. Included in the course were such subjects as respiratory diseases, intestinal diseases, venereal diseases, insect-borne diseases, housing of troops and military sanitation. So much in demand were qualified sanitary technicians that the nine-weeks course was reduced to seven weeks, later to six and then finally to four. Approximately 2,500 students attended the school.

Twenty hospital units were activated at Camp Ellis on May 25, 1943. Of this number, eight were station hospitals, three were ambulance companies, two were general hospitals, two were medical sanitary companies, one a field hospital, one a medical gas battalion, one a medical ambulance battalion, one a convalescent hospital and one a headquarters medical service. Exactly one month later, 12 more units were organized, among them, three medical sanitary companies. Activation was speeded up in August, and 20 more hospital units started training. For the first time Ellis saw Portable Surgical hospitals. The heaviest activation took place during the last month of 1943 when 79 units were prepared for training, the majority of them, malaria survey units, hospital trains, maleria control units and general dispensaries.

Civilians unfamiliar with the actual kind of training given in the various hospital units were guests of the Medical Group during Camp Ellis' 4th of July dedication ceremonies. The Medical Group exhibited a cross-section of the functions of the units, demonstrating techniques of first aid, erection and operation of ward and hospital tents,supervision of sanitary areas, proper gas mask drill, ambulance loading, and the operation of many other types of medical field installations.

One type of medical outfit which invariably aroused more than average interest among laymen and was unique in the training was the hospital train. An autonomous unit, the hospital train carried a compliment of forty enlisted men, six nurses and four medical officers, and was schooled to hospitalize the wounded on their journey to ports of homeward embarkation. Overseas the hospital-on-wheels is usually made up of 21 cars, one a kitchen, dining and pharmacy car, one a baggage-utility car and one for officers' quarters. Bedridden patients are carried on the lower tier of the doubledeck beds and ambulatory patients in the upper when the train is in actual hospital use.

Training was not easy for the medics. A thorough and efficient job had to be done in every unit in the Medical Group. Experienced and capable men were needed overseas and it was the job of the Medical Group to train raw recruits as quickly as possible for the all-important tasks awaiting them in com-

Setting up an Aid Station.

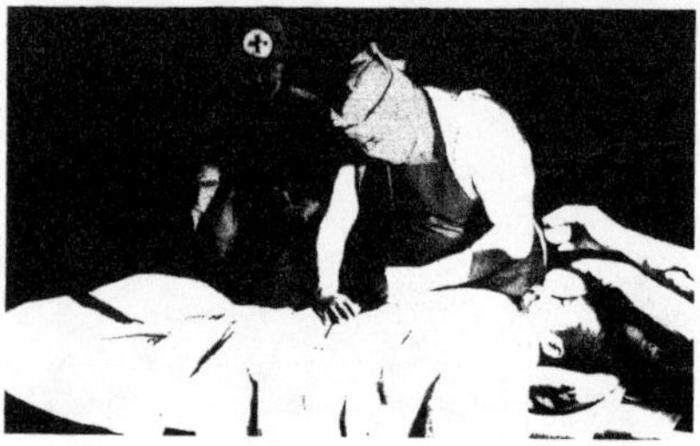

Wounded receive expert treatment.

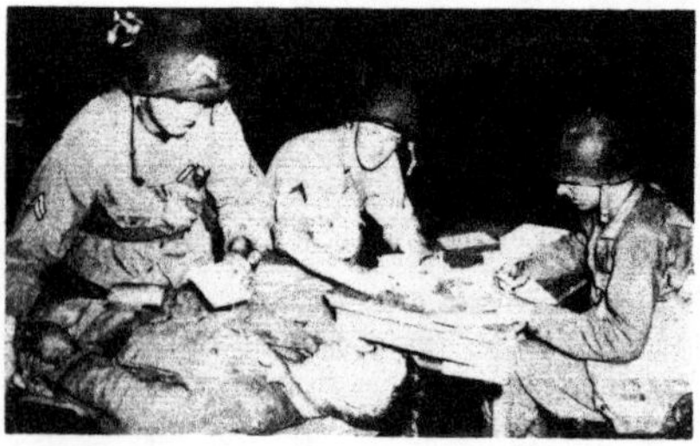

Medic Clearing Station.

Eating chow on bivouac.

bat theaters. This was especially true of soldiers in field hospitals. A field hospital is the nearest Army hospital unit giving medical treatment to front-line soldiers. Located four or five miles behind the fighting lines, this unit gives whatever treatment is indicated to surgical patients, then evacuates them to the rear as soon as possible. A field hospital is very mobile, very versatile. It can be used as a collecting station in forward areas or in the rear as a larger hospital. Medically, a field hospital is equipped to do anything a general hospital does. Its equipment can be transported in C-47 planes.

Typical of the many field hospitals that trained at Camp Ellis was the 62nd Field Hospital. Activated on 20 March 1944, the unit embarked on its rigorous training program. After a six-week basic training course, the men were sent to various Medical schools where they were given the opportunity to specialize. Eight weeks later the field hospital was ready for its first bivouac. During the time in the field each platoon had an opportunity to move the equipment once during the day and once under blackout conditions. In order to increase the efficiency of moving, each succeeding situation was made more difficult. Between moves —there were seven of them—training was maintained. A major problem stressed during the maneuver was the allocation of the available transportation to the various parts of the unit, so that it might be moved with the greatest of speed.

Highlight of the entire Medical Group training program was in October, 1944, when, for the first time in the history of the Camp Ellis Medical Group, a hospital unit participated in an airborne training maneuver. The unit was the 73rd Field Hospital under the command of Lt. Col. Robert E. Stokes. The maneuver got underway when four C-47 transport planes landed at the Camp Ellis airport after a flight from the First Troop Carrier Command at Stout Field, Indianapolis. Pitched nearby in quasi-bivouac fashion was the 73rd with equipment for the airborne operation packed and tagged and each jeep, trailer, cot, medical and dental chest ready for its proper spot in the plane. Designed to simulate field conditions the maneuver required the equipment of a headquarters and one of the three platoons of the field hospital, a total of 54,000 pounds.

The planes taxied into position on the landing strip. Chocks were dropped and loading crews began the operation. Loaded jeeps went up the ramps into two planes, loaded trailers into the other two; next the medical chests,

C-47s preparing for take-off.

Loading the C-47's.

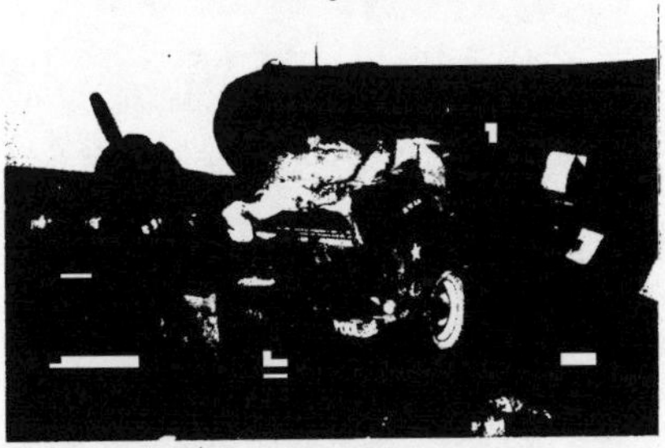

This time the jeep takes a ride.

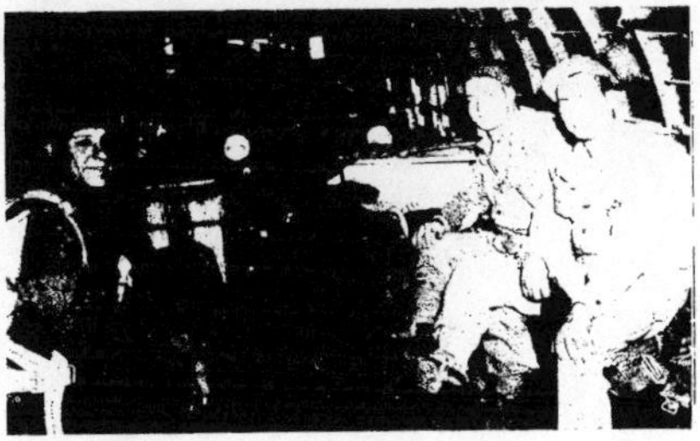

On their way.

ward tents, dental chests, pegs and poles. (Fuselage interiors are marked by inches and the total load is distributed so that the center of gravity during flight is between 250 and 256 inches from the nose of the plane). No time was lost in the loading operation, one of the planes being loaded in 20 minutes. Later, they unloaded at George Field, Ill., in 17 minutes. As the motors of the four transports were given a final warm-up, a fifth C-47 dropped out of the skies from George Field with a load of parachutes for the 73rd traveling crews.

Flying time from the bivouac area to George Field was 1 hour and 10 minutes. At the field, installation work progressed as scheduled.

When the Medical Group locked its doors Jan., 1945, one of the toughest and exacting mission in Army Service Forces training was completed. Training men to save others injured in combat has paid off with big dividends. Camp Ellis can look with pride to the 266 medical units activated here, most of which are now operating overseas. In closing, the attention of the reader is invited to the overseas section which tells of the work performed by some of these medical organizations in the battle areas.

Signal Group

THE chapter in our story of the Signal Group, like the group itself, is somewhat more brief but takes its place in comparative importance in the story as a whole. Like the Quartermaster Group, the history of the Signal Group does not start at Camp Ellis. All officers and enlisted men comprising the Signal Group were members of the Central Signal Corps Unit Training Center at Camp Crowder, Missouri. They had been assigned to this organization during the latter part of March, 1943. Their training at Crowder was rigorous and practical. It had to be. These signalmen were going to be responsible for the supervision of the entire training of all signal units at Camp Ellis.

When the Signal Group rolled into Camp Ellis on April 29, 1943, it was a well-trained, capable and efficient organization; and when the first Signal Corps unit arrived at the Illinois encampment the Group was well prepared and equipped to start at once the authorized training program and to furnish all training aids and equipment necessary to make the training effective.

Commanding the group was Colonel James E. Austin of New York City. A veteran of service on the Mexican Border, Colonel Austin also served in World

War I as a field artillery major with the 27th Division. He took part in the St. Mihiel and Meuse-Argonne offensives and was awarded the Silver Star decoration with Oak Leaf Cluster for gallantry in action. After the war he returned to inactive status as a reserve officer. He was called to duty July 17, 1942, and was assigned to the Aircraft Warning Service, Orlando, Florida. Colonel Austin took command of the Signal Group on June 4, 1943.

One battalion and four companies were the only Signal Corps units to train at Camp Ellis during the Group's short stay. They were the 297th Signal Installation Company, 246 Signal Operation Company, 244th Signal Operation Company, 188th Repair Company and the 35th Signal Construction Company.

Most signalmen at Ellis were thrown into action when the Illinois River and its tributaries overflowed their banks in May, 1943. The men were cited for their devotion to duty as they battled the flood side by side with Engineer and Quartermaster troops. The Signal Group, by supplying and operating portable radio equipment, enabled the commanding officer of the detachment to utilize with greater efficiency the forces at his disposal.

One of the most unforgettable incidents during the Signal Group Training at Camp Ellis—unforgettable but nevertheless a valuable lesson—occurred during a bivouac being conducted by the 297th Signal Company. While on field maneuvers the signalmen were taken completely by surprise by swift-striking Commandos as day was breaking. The Commandos, striking suddenly with tear gas and covered by dense smoke, threw confusion into the ranks of the entire company. The attackers deployed around a hill and silently crawled 1½ miles in the wet grass past the outposts and first cut all telephone communications. The half of the attacking force enveloped the command post in smoke and tear gas while the remaining Commandos turned the gas and smoke on the bivouac area. First to be captured were the commanding officers. The mock battle was the highlight of the maneuver and gave everyone valued experience in actual field practice.

One of the most colorful Signal outfits to train at Camp Ellis was the 297th Installation Company which at one time boasted only seven buck privates on its roster. The 297th was

Mobile Signal repair truck.

Linemen's Class at work.

the second installation company organized in the Army, the first landed with the Allies in North Africa. An installation company's job is to provide power, switchboards and "toll" equipment for the nerve center of a theater of operations. Armies, corps, separate units, other theater headquarters and even cities outside the theater may be connected to the central switchboard. An installation company's job stops when the equipment is in. They do not furnish the telephone operators or maintain installations. Nor do they have any equipment of their own except for tools.

This was the task that members of the 297th prepared for while at Camp Ellis. Other signal units maintained a more or less routine schedule stripped of any outstanding or colorful training happenings. Despite this, the men trained hard at their jobs with the knowledge that in combat areas the work of the signalmen in establishing and operating communications is vitally important in the successful prosecution of a campaign.

Organization and training of signal units at Camp Ellis did not last long. Most of the companies were out of the camp by August. Signal Group training came to an end on September 20, 1943, when the last of the units bade farewell to Camp Ellis.

Engineer Group

THE camp was by no means finished when the Engineer Group's advance party, headed by Col. Robert D. Ingalls and composed of 26 officers and 86 enlisted men, arrived on 28 April 1943. But what the Engineers don't find they build—and so they set about immediately to construct training areas and facilities in the space allotted to them. Training cadre units were scheduled to come in soon; time was short so not even the flood control emergency was allowed to slow down their program.

Colonel Ingalls, commanding officer of the group, was an Engineer officer of long, colorful experince and widespread reputation. Upon being graduated from Cornell University in 1917, he entered the Army and served in France with the Fifth Engineer Regiment. He continued his Army career at many stations in the United States and in Panama. He was executive officer of the 41st Engineer Regiment at Fort Bragg, North Carolina, in 1940. His was a colored organization which gained fame as the "Singing Engineers." In 1942 he organized and trained the 35th Combat Engineer Regiment for the important mission of constructing 250 miles of the Alaska Highway. His outstandbat conditions.

Before the advent of Col. Ingall's group, most of the administrative details were placed in the hands of Post Headquarters for it was felt that if the Engineer Group were relieved of such problems as housing, feeding, supply and other routine functions, more time could be devoted to the primary matter of training the units soon to arrive. This policy proved only partially successful, however, and it was evident that training and administration were too closely associated to be divorced completely. An Engineer headquarters was therefore organized to handle its own administration details, and it was under this setup that the advance party took over.

Much construction was necessary. Plans, blueprints and surveys were made for additional ranges, obstacle courses, bridges, construction areas and training sites. Shortly after the arrival of cadres for the first five units, the newcomers were put to work on this program. The five units were the 368th and 371st Engineer GS Regiments, the 447th Engineer Depot Company, the 573rd and 575th Engineer Dump Truck Companies.

These organizations were officially activated on 25 May 1943. From that date until the middle of August, they functioned at half their authorized strength because adequate personnel was difficult to obtain. Yet the situation gradually improved and by 1 September all these units were up to full strength. But another difficulty was more persistent—that of manpower quality in terms of physical fitness. It was discovered that only about 40 percent of the strength met general service standards. The other 60 percent had to be reclassified and reassigned.

The two phases of Engineer training were (1) general basic training for personnel of all units and (2) specialized training given smaller units according to their special assignments. All men were trained with the idea of functioning together as a well-

Bulldozer bogged down.

Bridging the Spoon.

knit team in combat areas. The length and types of special training depended upon the nature of each man's job. Basic and military training, combat principles, engineer construction and demolition work, and night operations constituted the principal subjects covered as the backbone of all training. In addition, about 40 per cent of the time was to be devoted to field operations of special types. Units adjudged standard in performance received six weeks of general basic training, seven more weeks of tactical and technical training and another three weeks of field problems—16 weeks in all. Sub-standard units received their six weeks of basic training, then continued with three weeks of reviewing their basic training. This was followed by 13 weeks of tactical and technical training and four weeks of field problems—a total of 26 weeks in all. Colonel Ingalls firmly believed in the value of firing practice as an aid to the improvement of marksmanship, and his theory proved correct if the records made by some 6,000 men are considered. Col. Ingalls estimated that 96 percent of the men qualified. Col. Ingalls also believed in stressing "a sense of urgency" in training practice—bearing down hard on training conditions and fitting the trainees for their actual battle missions. Although many men felt quite naturally that they were being pressed hard, letters received later from units overseas that had trained at Ellis testified to the correctness of this procedure, and the men who entered combat knew that their training, rigor-

Working on the railroad.

Blacksmith Class in session.

Plumbing Class at work.

ous as it may have been at this camp, was not as hard as the experiences they encountered in battle.

Schools for the development of skilled enlisted specialists were established to provide sufficient personnel for handling the many different technical duties that come under Engineer supervision. Schools were set up on a continuing basis, with permanent instructors. The instructors were under Group supervision at Headquarters. Approximately 60 schools were organized in this group. They were divided into four general sections: (1) construction schools, (2) heavy equipment schools, (3) shop schools and (4) miscellaneous schools. Under construction, the following schools operated: Carpenter, Electrician, Masonry

Masonry Class tests skill on Engineer Castle.

Loading heavy equipment.

Plumber-Pipe Fitter, Painter and Tool Room Keeper. In the heavy equipment schools, men were taught the use and care of all types of heavy equipment such as tractors, scrapers, concrete mixers, crane-shovels, ditchers, earth augers, graders, jack hammers, etc. The shop schools included the Blacksmith's school, Construction Equipment Mechanic schools and Welding School. Those under the miscellaneous category included Camouflage, Demolition, Rigging and Structural Steel.

Students were selected by unit commanders and were excused from other duties while in attendance. Instructor demonstration and student performance methods were chiefly used. The schools continued during the entire time that Camp Ellis was a unit training center.

In addition to regular schools, many other activities that formed a highly important part of the men's training were covered. Other jobs were undertaken—such as the removal of an abandoned 210-foot bridge across the Illinois river at Chillicothe and floating it down to Havana, 60 miles away, and the building of an air-strip at camp. These activities served as excellent "schooling" for the men. Maneuvers at Shawnee National Park further added to their training, and even operations carried out during flood control duty served to familiarize the men with the techniques involved, providing them with the experience of working as a team during an emergency.

Early in August of 1943, a realistic battle demonstration was staged by the Engineer Group on the Bernadotte area northeast of the camp. Thousands of spectators could witness both the obstacle area and the floating bridge training shows at the same time. While Company A of the 358th sang their regimental song, a squad from the 573rd Regiment put on a fancy drill exhihibition. A crew from Company D of the 371st, with two trucks and two "cats", erected a huge gin pole of the type used at Army loading docks. This giant Douglas fir pole was set up by means of a smaller 60-foot pole, with winches and cables. Due to wet ground, "cats" had to be used to anchor the trucks drawing the winches, but the entire operation was completed in 15 minutes. Announcers explained the use of the motorized general-purpose trailer repair shop with standard engineer tool sets. An officer stole the show by acting the part of a dumb private walking into booby traps, emphasizing thereby what not to do in such a circumstance. Light tanks slithered over fox holes at high speed, crashing into obstacles and lumbering over formidable barriers. But the tanks were finally stopped by obstacles built by Company F of the 371st. A mine crater was blown with a 400-pound dynamite charge; demonstrations were put on to show the use of grenades, bangalore torpedoes and a flame fougasse. In the area below the steel bridge over Spoon River, soldiers of the 1301st Engineers demonstrated the use of assault boats in crossings and races. Infantry support rafts were erected. The 368th shot an infantry foot bridge across the muddy Spoon, launched a portable Bailey Bridge, constructed a pneumatic pontoon bridge and a steel bridge capable of supporting a 25 ton load. And, of much interest to all spectators was the operation of the mobile water purification set, which sucked up the murky Spoon river fluid and processed it into clear, sparkling, cold drinking water. Transition firing by expert marksmen at targets 600 yards away on the range south of the bridge completed the day's demonstration, which was the first of a monthly series to be put on by the various training groups at Camp Ellis.

Suspension bridge across the Spoon.

During the flood period of the Illinois and Mississippi rivers in April and May of 1944, 3000 men in the Engineer Group battled to plug holes and stop

Flood duty in the spring of 1944.

the seepage with sand bags and "snow fences." Colonel Sullivan first ordered out a contingent of 500 men from the 1309th Engineer Construction Battalion. They arrived the next day at Ft. Chartres State Park, a short distance from the levees of the surging Mississippi. They were assigned to protect 15 miles of waterfront north and south of their headquarters. Men from the 1785th, the 1787th and the 1767th Engineer Parts and Supply companies participated in the flood control work along the Illinois at Beardstown and at Harrisonville, Valmeyer and Waterloo, Illinois. They worked all day long and all night while the rain frequently poured down in torrents. Rations were obtained from Scott Field and field equipment and supplies from the Engineer Depot at Granite City, Ill. Some of the farmers living in bottom lands were evacuated and their possessions were transported to higher ground. Soldiers crowded the small towns on the outskirts of the flooded area whenever off duty. At Waterloo, Ill., they were treated to free movies on their arrival. Hotels, restaurants and pubs did a brisk business. The men worked hard but they felt they were part of a fight that mattered and they liked it.

Two enlisted men were decorated with the Soldiers' Medal for heroism displayed during the flood. All men participating in the battle against the waters were highly commended for their valiant work by Lt. Colonel L. N.

Beard, Corps of Engineers, who at that time was executive officer of the Group. Many letters of praise were received from townspeople throughout the flooded area and official recognition from higher Army echelons also was received.

In order to train soldiers to work together successfully on a mission and to teach them the use of various engineer tools, a Construction Area was established on the U. S. highway skirting the camp. As early as 1943, men were being trained on a battalion and company basis 24 hours a day. Devices were built—targets, rifle racks and training appurtenances—by all units which were segregated for training at squad sites so that the squads might remain intact during the period. Ninety percent of the classes were given tasks to perform and these centered mainly about the construction of a model camp site which included the erection of five barracks, one mess hall, a latrine, a headquarters house, a warehouse and a water tank. Practice was obtained in carpentry, plumbing, sewerage, drainage, ditching, railroad construction, landscaping, surveying and electrical wiring. The Engineers maintained a high speed while performing their tasks. These men were being trained for work in combat areas where swift movements mean much in the success of any mission.

Flood control work was initiated at Camp Ellis under Col. Ingalls and it also was in full force at the time he was relieved of his command in May, 1944, and assigned to new duties at San Antonio, Texas. He was succeeded on 17 May by Col. Herman W. Schull, Jr.

Col. Schull, a West Pointer, had served as Engineer officer at various posts in the United States and in Hawaii. Prior to his coming to Ellis he had been commander of the Engineers of the 14th (China) Air Force under Major General Claire Chennault and had constructed many of its air bases in the China theater.

A reorganization of the internal administration of Headquarters in the Engineer Group was effected shortly after Col. Schull assumed command. He issued a memorandum outlining the changes on 19 June. The major changes were: first, the elimination of the Executive Officer as an intermediary between the different sections and the Colonel in command; second, the establishment of four, instead of the previous three, divisions in the group. The independent sections of Supply, Ordnance Vehicles and Engineer Equipment were combined into a new Materials Division to form the fourth division. The Training Status Section was renamed the Control Division and the Adjutant Section was named the Personnel Division. However, the functions of all sections remained the same. The major effect of the change was to bring the Commanding Officer into more direct touch with all activities of the Group. Control was decentralized into the major divisions with lines of responsibility clearly defined.

The Engineers signed out of Ellis on Jan. 25, 1945. Final tabulations at training headquarters credited them with putting 45 units in the field. These units endured training that was rugged and rough, and whatever the debates on the merits of this policy, reports from overseas units substantiated the sense of urgency that was a part of every Engineer's life from sun-up to sunset.

Wrote Col. Francis Purcell, CO, 1301st General Service Regiment — "Your training was exactly along the right lines; if anything, it should have been more so." From another battle area Col. Vincent I. Vanderburg, of the 1303rd General Service Engineer Regiment wrote — "We needed everything you gave us and a little more. I actually wish the training was stiffer."

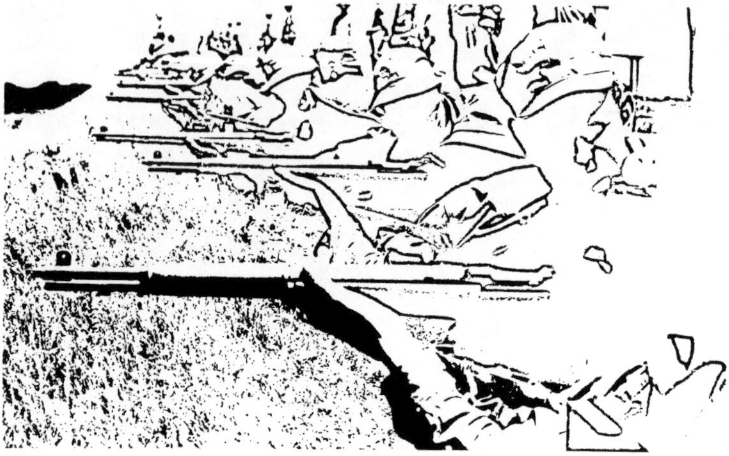

Training Group

THE Training Group, originally termed the Pre-activation Training Group, was established for the purpose of giving each man the required basic training and the technical training for his branch of the service before being assigned to a unit for overseas duty. During this phase of the training, rookies were separated from seasoned soldiers; and, through a special screening process, each man was fitted into an appropriate Army job. Men of special abilities were spotted and placed available to the service to which they were most readily adaptable.

Once the establishing order was issued, it may be said that the Group's life and activity was spontaneous. Lt. Colonel George Martin, the Group's first Commanding Officer, with a cadre of two assisting officers and 178 enlisted men began operations on the 24th of May, 1944, with a resolve that is best explained by their accomplishments.

The originally assigned area, bound by S and T Streets, 30th and 33rd—with 147 buildings and no equipment whatever—being received in an "off limits" condition, was not only prepared to receive the first contingent of 270 men, but the rate of influx was such that two hundred tents were pitched in this area. Eight buildings on 29th Street and six on 47th Street were utilized and ten other groups of fifty men each were located in other areas of the camp. Before the end of the first week the five companies of the First Training Battalion were inspected by the Inspector General of the Sixth Service Command, Colonel Joseph P. Aleshire. Each company, every one of which was commanded by a first sergeant, received a letter of commendation for the splendid showing made.

On the 5th of June, twenty-eight officers were attached temporarily to assist in training, eight of them from the Army Service Forces and twenty from the Army Ground Forces. Though a great part of the organization had been completed, their service was invaluable in launching the training program for the entire Group. Most of them left around the 1st of July for their permanent assignments.

The screening and processing was started on the 27th of May and only by long hours of hard work was the schedule maintained. Approximately 7,400 men were handled during the summer months. After screening, the Classification and Assignment Section, consisting of some fifteen enlisted men and one officer experienced in interviewing and classification, gave the men examinations to determine their special qualifications and military knowledge.

Since it was necessary, at the time, to provide as many men as possible for the Medical Group training in the camp, Lt. Colonel Austin P. Haller, the Executive Officer of the Group, coordinated all phases of administration and training between the Pre-activation Training Group and the Medical Training Group. Eighty-nine men were selected within the first week to be sent to various technical schools.

As the training progressed, eighty-two percent of the men qualified on the range and by the 7th of June the Second Training Regiment was organized, many of the men being temporarily housed in tents because by the 19th of June a total of 5,909 had been received.

By the end of June the First Training Regiment was completing their basic training and the Leadership School, organized under the direction of Colonel W. Lutz Krigbaum, became a part of the Training Group. Classes were started on the 4th of July. The course was designed to run three weeks and classes of approximately 100 men were started at the beginning of each week.

The purpose of the Leadership School is best given here by quoting the Camp Commander's letter of welcome to the students entering the school: "... You have been selected to attend this school because you have displayed those qualities which indicate leadership ability.... From a standpoint of society, the world may be divided into leaders and followers. All leadership is based on learning how to deal with men. It is in the military service where men freely sacrifice their lives for a faith, where men are willing to suffer and die for the right or the prevention of a great wrong, that we can hope to realize leadership in its most exalted and disinterested sense...."

And it was with this spirit of self-confidence, moral-ascendancy, self-sacrifice, paternalism, fairness, initiative, decision, dignity and courage, that the school provided for some 700 men a three-week course to bring those qualities to the fore, a course that is not to be found outside the Army.

Toward the close of August, Col. Martin was called for overseas duty and Col. Krigbaum was given the command of the Training Group. He appointed Major James M. Cunningham his Executive Officer. During September, the Group effected transfers of most of its men into Medical Units for their final polishing before leaving for "over there," and on the 5th of October, consolidated the First and Second Training Regiments into one to be drawn upon for minor replacements.

The Training Group was deactivated on Nov. 16, 1944, but its training functions were continued under the Office of the Director of Training at camp headquarters. Though the Training Group was short-lived, it performed its mission provided with the knowledge of a job well done.

Overseas

THIS chapter is about the sons of Ellis who have gone to war. At the request of the historical research section, Ellis-trained units overseas were asked to submit reports of their activities in the areas of operation. Within the limits of operational security, those units that were able, complied. A number of these reports, which merely represent a cross-section of the tasks assigned, are reproduced verbatim.

In a way, this chapter is a testimonial to the training the units received here, and insofar as censorship permits, tells the story of how this training was applied against the enemy. Of necessity, this narrative is incomplete, and not until the war is over can the epic gallantry of Ellis-trained troops be fully told.

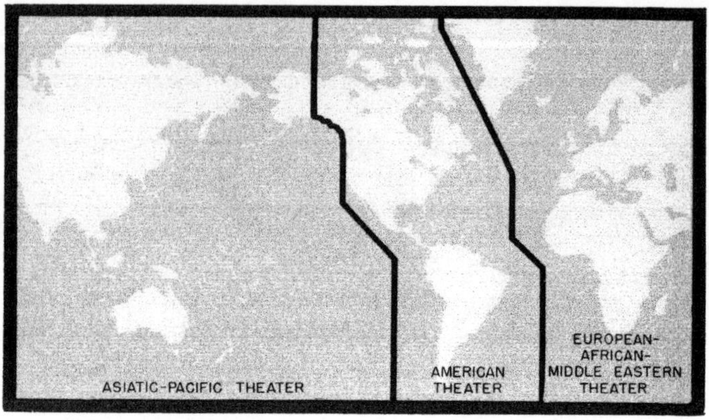

Reports from Overseas

FROM the training fields of Ellis to the battlefronts of the world have gone thousands of soldiers taught to perform specialized Army jobs – Medics, Engineers, Quartermaster, Signal Corps soldiers and others. Many of these reached Ellis as raw recruits from civilian life—eager lads from high school and college, men from farms and offices and industries all over America. As the largest ASF unit training center in the nation and one of the biggest Army camps in the midwest, Camp Ellis had been assigned a tremendous, all-important task—that of fitting these new, capable men into the right jobs and then providing them with the best possible training.

The intriguing story of the Camp itself and of the training programs carried out here has been briefly told in preceding pages. But one wonders, of course, just what success has attended this giant enterprise—this great Army expenditure of money, manpower, material and time. Has Camp Ellis succeeded in its primary mission? Has it given the soldiers it trained the needed knowledge, experience and confidence required to perform creditably in their overseas posts 'round the world? The answer can come only from those several hundred units themselves—from New Guinea and Guadalcanal, from the Solomons and other points in the Pacific, from Africa, Italy, the British Isles, from Normandy and even from inside Germany . . . . wherever these former Ellis trainees are on the job, putting into practice what they learned in the prairie lands of western Illinois, on the banks of the Spoon river.

Early in October, 1944, letters were sent out by the Camp Ellis Historical Research Section to every outfit that had received its training at this camp. The commanding officer of each unit was asked to tell briefly what his outfit had done since leaving Ellis, where they had gone, and a few of the interesting experiences they had had while performing their missions. Of course, it was felt that the percentage of replies would be small and that the material would be so carefully censored that many an exciting story would have to be omitted. This has proved to be substantially true, for, although more unit commanders responded than had been anticipated, many a first-hand account of a thrilling encounter with the enemy and many stirring tales of heroic work behind the front lines cannot now be related. Nevertheless, replies did come in from all theaters of operation and some of them traveled halfway 'round the world to reach Camp Ellis.

One report from a laundry unit in the Central Pacific arrived in a faded, water-logged condition "due to circumstances beyond control." What a thrilling story this manuscript might relate if only it could speak! Some of the reports were prepared with great care. (All unit histories received are being preserved in their entirety and have been placed among the permanent records of this Camp. They will eventually be turned over to the proper authorities in Washington.) Although only a few of the most interesting replies are here included—edited to leave out much routine material and censored information—sufficient history is at hand to emphasize the magnificent job that Ellis-trained soldiers are doing the world over.

As was expected, more replies were received from fixed or semi-permanent installations than from mobile outfits in the thick of battle. Numerous accounts have come in telling of the heroic, suicidal jobs performed by the Engineers. From a Signal Corps unit came a grand account of the part it played with the first wave of troops that invaded Normandy's shores. A QM Salvage unit in the South Pacific tells of unexpected fighting the minute it landed and then relates their experiences on the job — keeping their buddies properly equipped and clothed. Hospitals overseas tell of numerous difficulties overcome in getting set to care for sick and wounded and the everyday miracles performed in restoring fighting men to the front lines where they were urgently needed. Hospital trains traveled across former battle grounds up close to the front, evacuating and treating the wounded being returned to the zones of the interior and to waiting ships that would speed them home again. Malaria control units—tiny outfits—report from lonely outposts on South Pacific and Central Pacific Isles, and one unit tells of landing on Leyte. An Army Postal Unit that left Ellis less than a year ago has been with the swift-moving army of General Patton since June, streaking across France into Germany—and not content with handling more than three million pieces of mail in one month, reports the capture of 39 Nazi prisoners and of eating hot food left by the Germans in their headlong flight.

Many outfits will undoubtedly be heard from after this history has been printed. The following reports have been selected as typical of the work Ellis trainees are doing today, and even this handful gives ample testimony to answer the question raised by us at the outset. Let the record speak—clearly, emphatically, eloquently. It outlines the glowing deeds usually performed by young Americans, given expert training, the world's best tools with which to work, and a clear picture of what they are fighting for. The many personal deeds of valor in these units must await a later telling.

Pacific Theater

52nd Portable Surgical Hospital

"The 52nd Portable Surgical Hospital left Camp Ellis late in February, 1944. Our new station became Camp Robinson, Arkanas, here our training continued a short time before being alerted for overseas. Then came the multitude of inspections necessary prior to our movement. I must say the reflection of our training at Camp Ellis was one that brought very favorable comments from the Post Authorities. Inspector General and Eighth Service Command.

"Our POE was San Francisco and we staged from Camp Stoneman. The later part of April we departed on the U.S.S. ———, a new ship with fine accommodations.

"This ship stopped in Noumea, New Caledonia, for several days and then proceeded to Guadacanal, where we disembarked, early in May.

"While at Guadalcanal we ran a small dispensary, awaiting further orders. Late in July we received orders to move immediately by air, without equipment to Kwajalein. Our new mode of travel was enjoyable and made us all quite enthusiastic.

"At Kwajalein, our unit with another Portable Surgical Hospital, set up an annex to the already present Provisional Station Hospital.

"From here we were assigned on another mission, flew to another island where we later met our convoy. The food on this trip was excellent for all troops.

"This brings us to the Invasion of the Philippines, in which we had an opportunity to participate. We landed D plus one and on D plus two set up our station, functioned twenty-four hours alone and then became attached to a platoon of the Clearing Company of the 96th Division. With them we worked day and night for six days operating midst air attacks, bombings and constant artillery firing overhead. At night most of the time we had to operate with flashlights, but despite all obstacles I feel we did a very good job. The second week our work was much less and then followed a three week rest phase. The next assignment was with the 7th Division, functioning with the Clearing Platoons of Company D, 7th Medical

Battalion. We have handled all types of surgery and have carried out our mission successfully. We are still advancing with the Seventh Division."

539th Salvage Repair Company

"This company, activated and trained at Camp Ellis, has been overseas 10 months already, and through their activity as a combat outfit and a service unit, they have shown their mettle and proved their worth.

"Their stay in ———— lasted three weeks, during which time they served as labor troops working in warehouses, dumps, etc., aided in the building of roads and in the construction of various installations. . . . After three weeks, they again boarded a boat, this time to go to their final destination. They landed in March, 1944. . . . they discovered that they had come right in the middle of a concentrated Japanese push to recapture the American held perimeter. The company commander was immediately called upon to supply security and fire guards for ammunition dumps, oil storage areas, and ration dumps. These Quartermaster soldiers did their duty and walked their guard under definite combat conditions. Guard duty coupled with the fact that a company area had to be cleared out of thick jungle, living quarters—six pyramidal tents—had to be built, a mess hall erected, air raid shelters and foxholes dug—all this proved very trying to the company. But every individual soldier pitched in and worked hard uncomplainingly, and all the details required of them were fulfilled. . . . For this work, every member of the company was awarded the Asiatic-Pacific ribbon with the bronze combat star. This decoration was formally presented by the colonel in charge in the middle of April . . .

"By this time the operational equipment arrived and the company was ready to do the task it was specifically trained for—the task of salvaging and repairing of every kind of Army clothing and equipment. In record time, the shops were completed, machinery set up, electricity installed, and the company ready for business . . . a business that was sorely needed. For months the fighting jungle soldiers had been going around in worn shoes, torn clothing, and sleeping in torn leaky tents. There was an enormous stockpile of clothing and equipment that needed repair.

"In seven months of activity on ————, the shoe shop has handled approximately 100,000 pairs of shoes, an average of 600 pairs of shoes a day on a six-day work week. In addition, it has rebuilt about 700 pairs of shoes into orthopedic shoes for wounded and defective feet. All other kinds of leather such as pistol holsters, knife cases, baseball gloves, baseball shoes, footballs, punching bags, volley balls, and the like, also have been repaired. . . . Not all Army trade . . . a civilian clientele that boasted of such famous names as Frances Langford, Carole Landis, Bob Hope and Jack Benny. When pretty little Patty Thomas, a dancer with the Bob Hope USO troupe, brought in a pair of dancing shoes to be fixed, they were repaired with more than the usual amount of enthusiasm. As a matter of fact, some soldiers almost got Purple Hearts in the rush. . . . The clothing repair shop has averaged a turnover of 70,000 pieces of clothing a month . . .

"An innumerable amount of knapsacks, rifle belts, blankets, canteen covers, litter covers, and valpacks have found new life here. The field crew, often going up to the very front lines, inspecting and repairing tents, has averaged 3,500 tents a month. . . . 1500 sleeping cots monthly. . . . Altogether, the various sections of the 539th QM Salvage Repair Company have done a tremendous job. The saving in money to the government would register in the hundreds of thousands of dollars; but what is more important is the time factor. The fighting soldier need not wait for a ship from the "States" to bring him new clothes, shoes and equipment. Here, right on the spot, and in a couple of days he can get his material back as good as new. The amount of shipping space saved this way is also a factor. The important work of this company has been recognized and acknowledged by officers all the way up the line. . . ."

85th Malaria Survey Unit

"This organization left Camp Ellis 23 March 1944 for Camp Plauche, La. . . . arrived at Camp Stoneman, California, 7 June and departed for overseas service. . . . Arrived at Oro Bay, New Guinea, 18 July. . . . This unit had the honor of accompanying the first task force to invade the Philippine Islands. . . . Arrival on Leyte was made A-4, 24 October 1944. This organization, immediately upon landing, undertook the survey of a large part of the area which our troops had occupied. The most immediate problems were to determine: The malaria problem, malaria mosquito breeding, the dengue fever problem, dengue mosquito breeding, and a new problem which our forces in this theater had never faced—the Schistosomaisis problem. During the early period of occupation, this organization was continuously bombed and strafed but no casualties were suffered."

37th Field Hospital

This outfit trained at Ellis from May, 1943, until February, 1944, and left in full strength for a California port of embarkation. It arrived at its destination in the South Pacific early in March.

"The climate is very hot and humid . . . . one of the heaviest annual rainfalls in the whole world . . . . the area is flat, well drained, shaded by cocoanut palms. Under sunlight it becomes uncomfortably warm, even while raining. The nights are cooler, making it possible for troops to sleep well.

"At this date of writing this unit is still up to T/O strength. There have been no losses of personnel either by evacuation or by casualty in combat.

"The majority of enlisted men have been employed since March in construction work either in our own bivouac area or on neighboring installations that are building permanent hospitals.

"The housing of personnel has been in pyramidal tents. Since the unit is staging, no wards or surgeries have been set up. A unit dispensary has been set up in a pyramidal tent. Eventually this unit will use squad tents for wards when it goes into operation."

Another unit: "In order to lay out the hospital and living quarters for the personnel it was necessary to clear virgin jungle underbrush. An Engineer unit on several occasions made available a bulldozer. The insect life is rather heavy—spiders, ants and flies being present in great number.

"Fresh water is used to bathe patients but medical department personnel make use of the adjacent beach for bathing purposes. . . . Separate kitchens are operated for patient and medical department personnel, the former getting such choice foods as are available. Canned rations are used to a great extent for medical department personnel but are prepared as tastefully as possible. . . . Patients are fed on plastic trays. Unit personnel use the GI mess kit. . . . No tables for mess, therefore eating is decidedly an informal procedure.

"During one week there were 325 patients admitted to this hospital . . . of these 301 were battle casualties and 24 non-battle casualties.

"All personnel performed very well despite the fact that on the occasion of this unit's first beginning to function as a hospital, we were extremely hard pressed by the rate of admissions."

567th Engineer Dump Truck Company

"On 24 February 1944, this unit departed from Camp Ellis by rail with a strength of four officers and one hundred and ten enlisted men, and arrived at Camp Stoneman, California on 9 March 1944, embarked ou the ship that was to carry us to our overseas destination. Blackout security was strict and abandon ship drills were held several times a day until satisfactory all clear was accomplished and the Captain was satisfied that the troops were sufficiently trained. The trip was uneventful except when another ship was sighted at night and then everyone sighed with relief when it was ascertained to be friendly. Nearby carrier based planes provided security and on several occasions towed targets for our gun crew to practice. Much confidence was placed in them as their aim proved excellent.

"On 27th March our ship anchored in harbor outside New Caledonia . . . and arrived in New Guinea 3 April 1944.

"During June, July and August we hauled cargo from the docks and gravel for various projects, the hauling at the Gurney airstrip reconstruction, being valuable training, was by far the biggest job we have handled to date."

334th Station Hospital

"This organization departed from Camp Ellis on January 18, 1944 . . . landed at New Guinea. In mid-summer of 1944 moved to an advance base in the Netherlands East Indies and the construction of the hospital began in a scenic location on a high bluff overlooking the Pacific ocean. For the most part the patients have been battle casualties from the East Indies and Philippine Islands Campaigns . . . The training which this unit received at Camp Ellis from August, 1943, until January, 1944, has been invaluable in the accomplishment of our mission in this overseas theater."

41st Field Hospital

Left Camp Ellis 25 October 1943 . . . took a two weeks training course in airborne operations at another camp in United States . . . arrived at Camp Butner, N. C., 8 November by motor convoy . . . spent three months in intensive training, then left this country on 18 February 1944 . . .

"Approximately three weeks later, 13 March 1944, we landed at Milne Bay, New Guinea, where for five months the unit staged, set up and operated a portion of the operating section to reacquaint the personnel with the intricacies of the equipment and provided labor details for the construction of general hospitals and general detail. On 7 August, flew with equipment to Biak Island . . . difficulties were encountered . . . forced to move. . . . An area was cleared, tents thrown up and the first patient registered on the 25th of August, 1944. The remainder of the organization arrived by boat on I September and the nurses on the 27th of September. . . . In two months of operation this unit has cared for 3,310 patients, at times with a census of 50 percent above T/O bed capacity. The Base Surgeon sent this organization a letter of commendation for work performed at this base. . . . While at Biak Island this unit was subjected to approximately 15 air raids, but suffered no casualties. At present all equipment has been packed in readiness for the impending move to new scenes of operations."

205th Malaria Survey Unit

"After leaving Camp Ellis the unit went to Camp Plauche, La., for advanced training in malaria work both in the field and laboratory.

"Camp Stoneman, California, was the next stop before leaving for overseas. The trip enroute to New Guinea took almost one month, and after arrival, four months were spent in a staging area to acquaint the men with work already done and work to be done in the future.

"The unit left the staging area and arrived at a more advanced base in Dutch New Guinea, joining the 24th Infantry Division and embarking for the invasion of the Philippine Islands.

"Five hours after the initial landing on 20 October 1944, A-Day, the unit splashed up to the beach for their first engagement with the enemy. So far as can be ascertained this was the first malaria survey unit ever to land on A-Day and the first Malaria Unit to land during this operation. To date there have been no casualties in the unit. Aside from air raids and constant movement the biggest problem we have had to contend with has been enemy snipers.

"Surveys have been made of native diseases which might affect troops. The unit is also participating in sanitary work in the different localities where the Division troops are bivouacked."

759th Medical Sanitary Company

"This company left Camp Ellis 12 April 1944, arrived at Fort Francis E. Warren, Wyoming, 15 April. . . . We do not intend to praise ourselves, but due to the high technical training this unit received from the Medical Department at Camp Ellis, the malaria lectures were so well given to a group of field officers that the commanding officer received a letter of commendation. A copy of this letter was forwarded to the Medical Group Headquarters at Camp Ellis. . . . Furloughs before going overseas were given. . . . Since our arrival in this theater we have been working jointly with field, station and general hospitals also trained at Camp Ellis and who are doing a swell job taking care of battle casualties from the Philippines. . . . We know that Camp Ellis is behind us because each day we see a unit and the majority of them all praise Ellis for the high technical training received there. We are trying to show our gratitude by doing a good job over here."

72nd Malaria Control Unit

"This unit departed from Camp Ellis 28th February, 1944, for Camp Plauche, New Orleans, La. . . . Arrived at Camp Patrick Henry, Va., 16 April 1944. . . . At sea from 22 April to 10 May 1944. . . . Staged at Oran, Algeria . . . departed from Oran 12 May 1944 . . . at sea from 12 May to 1 June. . . . Arrived at Bombay, India 1 June . . . duty in India from 20 June to 3 July . . . assumed duties of Malaria Control Work of air bases of —— Bomber Command . . . three bases . . . on 4 July 1944. . . . No pictures available at this time . . ."

738th Engineer Base Depot Company

". . . departed from Camp Ellis 1 April 1944 . . . arrived at Granite City Engineer Depot in Illinois same date . . . underwent further training . . . departed from port of embarkation 1 July 1944 . . . arrived in New Guinea 31 July . . . assigned to work in the UNASOS Engineer Base Depot. . . . This unit has since assumed operation of the depot headquarters and yard operations. Men are engaged in depot administration, crane operation and maintenance, checking, warehousing, and motor maintenance and operation. . . . This unit was reorganized 30 May 1944, per order from Headquarters, Armed Forces in the Far East. . . . This unit is now looking forward to its part in coming operations in this theater."

85th Malaria Control Unit

"This unit was activated at the ASFUTC, Camp Ellis, Illinois, 10 December 1943.

"The crossing was uneventful with the exception of the initiation of the troops into the Shellback Club during the crossing of the Equator. On 22 June 1944 the ship docked at Finschhaven, New Guinea. Here the unit debarked and was attached to the 134th General Hospital for rations and quarters.

"Approximately two weeks after arriving at Finschhaven, a Malaria Control Unit was asked to volunteer to go into operation at Saidor, New Guinea. This unit volunteered to undertake this job.

"Setting up operations were finished in

three days and on 15 July 1944, actual Malaria Control operations were started. This work consisted in spraying streams and stagnant water, cutting kunai grass, and clearing areas and streams. This work was done with the aid of approximately forty natives daily, who were obtained from ANGAU, at ——, the Malaria rate was low."

From A Portable Surgical Hospital

"Departed Camp Ellis, 23 February 1944.

"Departed Continental United States on 22 April 1944 and arrived at APO 709 on 12 May 1944. Attached to 48th Station Hospital for duty.

"Departed APO 709 7 August 1944 and assigned to USS Mercy for duty 16 September 1944.

"A number of voyages have been made participating in the treatment and evacuation of war casualties from the Philippine Theater."

58th Portable Surgical Hospital

This hospital was officially activated on 15 August 1943 . . . on 25 October it left for the port of embarkation on the east coast. . . . "Two days out at sea this unit performed an emergency appendectomy on board a Liberty ship . . . probably one of the first instances in which major surgery was performed on this type of vessel. . . . After a short stay in North Africa . . . went to India and in upper Assam assisted in processing Chinese troops. At the beginning of the campaign the hospital was flown into Burma. After moving on foot through Jap infested territory the installation was established in the front lines in support of the American troops. Since the hospital was less than 200 yards from the Japanese lines it was repeatedly subjected to artillery and mortar fire plus the occasional Japanese soldier stealing his way through the American perimeter. One such an individual actually crawled up to the hospital one night, but fortunately decided to commit suicide and did so, holding a hand grenade to his chest. . . . To afford as much protection as possible to the hospital, the operating room was heavily sandbagged and surgery after darkness was performed under the strictest of blackout conditions. In spite of these precautions it was repeatedly necessary to place the patients on the ground and continue surgery there, to make a smaller target for enemy shell fire. . . . Doing major surgery on one's knees using nothing but hand-held flashlights for illumination was certainly a new experience for the medical officers. After the campaign the unit moved south and at present is supporting Chinese forces. The 58th Portable Surgical Hospital has had some unusual experiences. It has traveled by plane, by train, by oxcart, by river barge, by pack horse and on foot. It has lived in foxholes and has functioned right with front line infantry troops. It has furnished definitive surgical treatment under the most adverse conditions, but has the satisfaction of feeling that it has fulfilled its purpose. It has done a job."

European Theater

50th Army Postal Unit

"The 50th Army Postal Unit left Camp Ellis on 16 February 1944 . . . after arrival in England, assigned to the —— Corps . . . participated in the training program . . . proceeded to a marshalling area and embarked on a Liberty ship for France. When the ship anchored off the coast of France all personnel and equipment were transferred to LCT's. The unit was split up into three sections . . . a severe storm broke that day and the LCT's maneuvered back into quieter waters until after the storm passed. This storm delayed our arrival in France several days. . . . Two sections arriving in France set up the equipment and had our first field APO operating when the last group of men arrived. The Corps then took the position of the spearheading corps of the Third Army and made a spectacular march through France . . . one of the fastest sustained marches in history. . . . The 50th APO during this period became a mobile post office—packing and loading equipment within a very few hours and setting up and operating in the same length of time. Only one mail dispatch was missed during the march through France and this was because of transportation difficulties. . . . Large groups of Germans were often trapped behind the fast moving front and on one occasion the 50th APO captured 36 Germans. Three more prisoners were taken by two men of the unit who were hauling mail, bringing our total up to 39 prisoners. . . . Lost two men as non-combat casualties. The 50th APU has participated in the campaigns of Normandy, Northern France and Germany . . . was the first APO across the Seine river . . . first across the Marne river . . . biggest field APO in France during the month of September . . . handled total of more than three million letters during that month . . ."

137th General Hospital

"The 273rd Station Hospital departed from Camp Ellis 6 September 1943. . . . proceeded to the Hospital Area, CZ, ETOUSA. After completing orientation course for ETO, unit was ordered to relieve a General Hospital operating at ———. This was accomplished 12 July 1944. Since that time we have functioned at our primary mission, that of a general hospital. We have received and evacuated all types of battle casualties from every combat area of France, Holland, Belgium, and Germany, by air and rail. This unit has been the recipient of many compliments for the manner in which the tasks assigned have been accomplished . . . these compliments are largely due to the superior type of enlisted men in the unit and the training they received, part of that training which was received at your station."

476th Military Police Escort Guard Company

"This organization was the first such outfit to arrive at Camp Ellis to handle prisoners of war, 11 August 1943. . . . Since leaving Ellis on 29 January 1944, this organization has been guarding and escorting PW's in the United States, the United Kingdom and on the continent of Europe. . . . Our transporting of prisoners include travelling by truck, rail and boat. . . . This organization participated in the Campaign of Northern France. . . . There are no clippings or magazines mentioning this unit or any available pictures."

13th Hospital Train

NOTE: The Commanding Officer of this Unit submitted a most extensive resume of the history and operations of his unit since its activation at Camp Ellis. They participated in the invasion of the continent and the copious report is of such interest that it has been rewritten here only to condense it. It has been used verbatum as the quotations indicate.

"Organized at Camp Ellis, 10 December 1943. . . . departed 3 May 1944 . . . and arrived in Scotland 23 May. Stationed as Medical Staff aboard British Hospital Carrier" 28 May and went on Operational status 5 June, D-Day minus 1 . . . "first operational mission was medical support and evacuation of wounded from the Coast of France. From 'D Day' to present date Unit has continued . . . performing operational missions."

Quotations from the daily operational log are:

"Boarded" carrier at ————. "Morale excellent."

"Arrived off ————, France . . . Halted at sea by Naval Craft following mining of '————' and '————' traveling in same group."

"Remained at anchor over night off ———— and were subjected to very heavy Air Raids throughout the entire night . . . proceeded to position off ———— and anchored . . . Began loading and treatment of casualties . . . despite heavy air activity, flak and shrapnel."

"Continued loading and treating casualties. Heavy enemy air activity continued Bombs dropped from enemy planes approximately 50 yards off port bow of ship. No damage sustained by patients, personnel or ship. Ceased loading . . . and proceeded . . . with full load of patients."

"Loaded ship to twice her capacity for patients, utilizing all available space for patients including Medical Staff quarters."

"Subjected to very heavy air raids at —— hours. Dive bomber dropped 3 bombs in water near starboard side of vessel. No damage sustained by personnel or ship. Began loading casualties at —— hours. Completed loading casualties and weighed anchor at (same time).

On returning to France . . . "strong North Easterly gale encountered lasting four days."

"Prior to leaving ———— Sector, unit and ship area had been submitted to heavy air raids for four successive nights. Vessel was not attacked. Observed enemy aircraft brought down nearby by anti-aircraft fire."

"Summary: During the operational period, 6 June 1944 to 30 September 1944, this Unit completed 16 medical operational missions to the Coast of France and accomplished medical evacuations and treatment totaling 3,795 patients" (American and British). "Unit participated in 'Battle of Western Europe' departing from the United Kingdom for France on 'D' Day and arriving in Operational Area on 'D plus one.' Unit has performed mission under enemy action, however no direct attacks were made upon this vessel and no casualties of personnel were sustained.

"Members of Unit on duty during month of June entitled to wear one service star on European African Middle Eastern Theater ribbon for participation in 'Battle of Western Europe'."

"The following letter of Commendation was received by Blinker Signal at ——— Normandy Beachhead from (Hq. Ship) to (our ship):

"We greatly appreciate the work you are doing and wish to express our thanks to the entire ship's company and staff in helping and for wholehearted co-operation. (Signed) Admiral Moon, USS ———, Hq."

"The work and function of this unit has been pictured and described in 'Collier's' 6 August 1944, article "The Wounded Come Home" and 'Stars and Stripes' warweek supplement, 20 July 1944, London Edition, article: "Fighting Yanks Aces With Nurses."

"During the month of October, 1944, this unit completed eight operational missions and accomplished medical evacuation and treatments totaling 2,731" (American and British).

246th Signal Operation Company

"Left Camp Ellis 1 September 1943. . . . Applied field problems for 14 weeks at Camp Edison, N. J. . . . by 12 February 1944 the unit disembarked at ———, Wales; proceeded by rail to ——— Worchester, where our mission proved to be operation of communications for the 8th Corps. . . . As of 24 March our assignment changed as follows:—assigned to 1st U. S. Army. A convoy of company vehicles was used to transport both personnel and equipment. Duty at this station was to assist the 17th Signal Operation Battalion to operate communications for the 1st U. S. Army.

". . . participated in the invasion of France landing at ———, Normandy, on D Day up to D Day plus 6 . . . mission was to install, operate and maintain signal communications at Third U. S. Army Forward Echelon. To accomplish all these missions, this company was divided into two sections. . . . Up to the present time this company has participated in three campaigns and received awards of Bronze Star for one officer and one enlisted man for meritorious service in connection with military operations on 7 June 1944."

119th General Hospital

". . . ordered into active service on 8 March 1944 at Camp Ellis . . . debarked and entrained to ———, England. Up to the present time there have been no further changes of station.

"The area at ——— formerly was the site of a British militia camp, converted to meet the needs of the hospital. Living quarters were established in the existing buildings comprising six wooden barracks and two Neisen huts for the enlisted personnel, two wooden buildings for officers, and three wooden buildings were assigned to the nurses. . . . Recreation facilities on the post included a movie theater with attractions changing twice weekly, a post theater where stage productions were held at least three nights weekly, a small library, and some very excellent athletic fields. . A reconditioning and rehabilitation program for patients was instituted on 18 September 1944, and consisted of calisthenics, lectures, drills, crafts, and viewing films.

"The first contingent of patients, numbering 295 and including some 20 members of the Allied armed forces, arrived on 13 August 1944. This group arrived by train. . . . Only seven were medical cases, the remainder being either general surgery or orthopedic cases. This mass admission was accomplished in one hour and fifty minutes. Litter teams composed of 96 men worked feverishly to bear the patients to assigned wards. Particularly busy were the personnel of the Receiving and Evacuation office and the Registrar's Department who worked the entire night and the greater part of the following day to get the records in order.

"During the period 13 August to 30 September 1944, a total of seven mass admissions were accomplished, each succeeding one with increased efficiency. A total of 886 admissions were reported during this period, 519 being surgical, 259 orthopedic, 86 medical, and 22 neuro-psychiatric cases. Of this total, 36 were members of other Allied forces. During the same period, there were 203 departures from the hospital, 123 being returned to duty, 44 transferred to other hospitals for further observation and treatment, and 36 returned to the Zone of the Interior. On 30 September 1944, the total number of remaining patients was 683. . . . Patients received at this hospital, in practically all cases, were in excellent condition, major surgery having been performed efficiently in hospitals along the route of evacuation. The work of the surgeons at the evacuation and field hospitals was most satisfactory, because very little major surgery was called for at this hospital—most of the work at this unit being confined to secondary closure of wounds. The wonders of the miracle drugs, penicillin and the sulfa compounds, were most outstanding. . . . The low incidence of neuropsychiatric cases received at this headquarters is explained by the fact that most such cases were sent directly to specialized hospitals in the United Kingdom. . . . A fact most noteworthy of mention was the absence of any deaths in this hospital. Another outstanding feature pointing to the successful handling of patients was the low percentage of evacuees to the Zone of the Interior."

590th Quartermaster Salvage Repair Company

"After being in France for about thirty days the Unit set up in a QM Depot. Since that time it has been recognized by the Area Commander as one of the best all around units in the command. At present the unit is servicing two crack Camp Ellis trained Salvage Collecting Companies. We serve all units on the St. Lozare-Laurent Salient. We handle thousands of garments per day, hundreds of pairs of shoes, textile equipment, typewriters, field ranges and other equipment. In addition the unit has been assigned operation of a parts warehouse. They clean their rifles twice each week and wait for orders. In case the Jerries get loose up front, the unit believes it has a special method of handling them."

125th General Hospital

"On 15 July 1944 the unit entrained from Camp Ellis, and . . . departed for overseas destination on 24 July 1944.

"The unit arrived at Liverpool, England, and entrained on 1 August 1944, for Dorset, England, arriving the same day.

"Evans Area, Blandford Camp, to which the unit had been assigned, was still in the process of being converted when the personnel arrived.

"The various departments were then located in specific buildings and the task of preparing the area for reception of patients was begun.

"On 20 August 1944, the Hospital was officially opened with a capacity of five hundred beds. This represented the total bed space available on that date, the remainder of the hospital still being in process of completion.

"The first patients arrived at the Hospital on 21 August 1944, via Hospital Train. The bed capacity of the Hospital was extended to 1,154 by 24 September 1944.

"On 30 August 1944 the first patients were received by Air Evacuation direct from Continental Europe. At the end of the month there were 328 patients.

"Throughout the month of September continued progress was made towards preparing the hospital to operate at maximum capacity.

"Recreation for enlisted men was made a matter of prime import. By this time, there was available for the use of the enlisted men a day room gymnasium adequately equipped for various athletic functions, tennis courts, a snack bar, a unit dance band and dances twice monthly.

"During this month the unit Officers' Club was officially opened and adequate recreation was made available to both officers and nurses.

"The Post Office received on the average 150,000 letters and 3,000 packages a month and sent out 60,000 letters and 1,000 packages a month.

"Awards of 373 Purple Heart Medals and 42 Oak Leaf Clusters were made by 30 September 1944."

1303rd Engineer General Service Regiment

"Regiment departed Camp Ellis, Illinois, 9 March 1944, via railroad for Boston and embarked at the POE 23 March 1944. The crossing in a large convoy was uneventful with ideal weather and with few exceptions the voyage was enjoyed by all. Arrived in Scotland, 3 April and proceeded by rail to Melchbourne Park, Riseley Beds, Bedfordshire, England. Till the 17th June, the regiment operated under the District Headquarters in various construction including roads and buildings and reconstruction of bombed facilities. On that date the regiment was attached to the ——— U. S. Army and eventually debarked in France before the end of July 1944. Continuing the same type of work with the addition of water supply, the regiment moved up with the ——— U. S. Army and at the present time is still in operations and owes much of its success to the training we received at Camp Ellis."

NOTE: The communication received from this regiment was the most comprehensive and exhaustive report to arrive up to the time of publication (124 pages) and a few of the photographs accompanying it have been included here.

103rd General Hospital

"The entire personnel of the 103rd General Hospital proceeded immediately after landing in the United Kingdom to its present site of operations, a British installation of over 100 buildings converted from former

A mud-bogged road before . . . .

. . . . the Engineers improved it.

The site before the construction . . . .

. . . . and after completion of bridge.

Army barracks. Within 10 days after the arrival of personnel the hospital went into operation with the arrival of battle casualties from the fighting on the continent of Europe. Seven weeks later the bed capacity was more than doubled. The 103rd General Hospital is the second largest in the United Kingdom."

11th Hospital Train

"This Unit left Camp Ellis on 3 May 1944, departing for overseas, landing in Scotland on 23 May 1944.

"After proceeding to England from Scotland, we again made a short sea voyage to the Continent.

"On 1 August 1944, with an improvised Hospital Train, this Unit became the first unit of its type to operate on the continent. The train was composed of French box cars in which emergency equipment had been installed. The box cars were the famous World War I "40 & 8." For the operation of this improvised hospital train this Unit received a commendation from the Surgeon, Normandy Base Section and from the Chief Surgeon, European Theater of Operations. In addition to the commendation, the Army newspaper, Stars and Stripes, printed an article concerning the train, and various newspapers in the United States printed pictures and stories about it.

"Since its arrival overseas this Unit has participated in three campaigns: Normandy, Northern France and Germany.

Quotations from Commendations.

"It is the desire of the Surgeon, Normandy Base Section, to commend you and the members of your command on the exemplary manner in which you have carried out your mission. Your Train Crew was the first one to reach the continent, arriving on 18 July 1944. From ——— you operated a provisional box-car type of train for ——— trips, and only since ——— have you had a standard Hospital Train. During the period of time that you operated this provisional train you transported ——— patients under the most adverse conditions. Officers, Nurses and EM lived and worked under very trying conditions, frequently transporting many more patients than the train was set up for and often having as many as 60 per cent seriously wounded patients. Delays in schedules, inability to get from one box car to another except when the train was stopped, frequent overloading, unsuitable living conditions. particularly for nurses, were among the problems encountered and overcome by your unit.

"In spite of all the difficulties encountered in the operation of this provisional train, your unit carried out its duties in an efficient, capable manner, at all times exhibiting cheerful optimism in the face of all obstacles, and delivering these thousands of patients to their destination without a single fatality.

"It is felt that the example you and your subordinates have set brings great credit to the Medical Department and is according to the highest traditions of the Military Service."

/s/ R. E. DUKE, Lt. Col., MC,
Surgeon.

"The Chief Surgeon, (HQ, ETOUSA) desires to add his commendation to that of the Surgeon, NBS. Your Hospital Train Unit has performed in an exemplary manner under adverse conditions and has helped to maintain the high standards of the Medical Service in this Theater."

/s/ PAUL R. HAWLEY, Maj.-Gen. USA,
Chief Surgeon.

297th Signal Installation Company

"Staged at Camp Shanks, New York, September, 1943.

"Arrived in the United Kingdom, October, 1943.

"Unit assigned to Headquarters, Service of Supply, to assist the British General Post Office in the installation of exchange facilities, both telephone and teleprinter, at military installations. Under the direction of the Chief Signal Officer. SOS. the following projects were completed: (Here are innumerated some 122 position installations, a 200 mile dial exchange, approximately one hundred speaking and keyboard sets, telephone repeater offices and additions to various facilities utilizing both American and British equipment.) Installations were made at US Army establishments, British Army establishments, USAAF Fields, RAF Fields, US Navy and the maneuver area in the UK.

"Unit reassigned to Advance Section, Communications Zone in April, 1944, and has operated under the direction of that headquarters to the present date.

"The operations of the unit since arrival on the continent (D plus 30) are: Initial installation of the telephone central for ASCZ and 3 subsequent installations as the headquarters advanced, rehabilitation of the Cherbourg civilian exchange which had been damaged during the capture of that port. (Here are innumerated some 47 position installations, and a number of repeater station installations utilizing both captured German equipment and French equipment where it could be salvaged and repaired, otherwise all the equipment used was American), installations were made by the unit in all base sections in Northern France and Belgium.

"This unit was operating in the European Theater of Operations within the time and geographical limits to be entitled to battle participation credit for the Normandy Campaign, The Northern France Campaign, and the Germany Campaign."

22nd Hospital Train

"The period 12 June 1944 to 31 July 1944 inclusive, was spent on DS with the ——— General Hospital, U. S. Army. Personnel were again assigned to regular Military Occupational Specialties. A letter of commendation is inclosed from Rawley E. Chambers, Colonel, MC, Commanding Officer of the ——— General Hospital, U. S. Army, for the splendid manner of performance of duty of all members of this command during the period stated . . . ("at a time of an acute personnel shortage.")

"On 13 September 1944, prior to departure from the United Kingdom for France, Hospital Train No. ——— was taken over by this organization. The first Operational Run was made in France on 9 October 1944. At this writing, thirty-one Operational Runs have been completed evacuating sick and wounded from the combat zone. Entrainment of patients in several instances has taken place while cities of entrainment were subject to heavy action."

569th Engineer Dump Truck Company

"Upon leaving Camp Ellis for overseas duty the organization embarked from Camp Shanks, N. Y., on 1 January 1944, and debarked in Scotland on 10 January 1944. After reaching a de-staging area in Southern England, the outfit joined the 389th Engineer General Service Regiment for training and work. The work consisted of hauling engineer construction materials for camp sites, helping clear bomb ruins, and road construction in Southern England.

"Work lasted with this engineer regiment until the middle of April 1944, when at this time the organization was attached to the 171st QM Truck Bn. . . . Commendations were given the company for its excellent driving record.

"By this time the 'Invasion' had shortly begun, so the organization was ordered to prepare for Continental duty, being relieved thereby, from the 171st QM Truck Bn., and assigned to the Advance Section Communications Zone.

"After landing in France on 8 July 1944, (D plus 32), the company was attached to the 374th Engineer General Service Regiment and hauled engineer materials and supplies for the construction of the first general hospital on the Continent. This work was accomplished while the enemy still bombed, shelled, and strafed the area around. During this time also the outfit was ordered to furnish trucks for hauling ammunition up to the front during the big drive early in

August.

"The outfit has credit both for the "Normandy Campaign" and the "Northern France Campaign." The fact that the organization has been rated as the third most efficient dump truck company in this theater adds much to the pride of the officers and enlisted personnel."

291st QM Refrigeration Company—Mobile

"This organization departed from Camp Ellis, Ill., 11 August 1944 and arrived in England 31 August 1944. Arrived in France 27 September 1944. The organization, almost immediately, started operations of its primary mission of hauling perishables from beach to inland cities and from depots to the front lines.

"This organization has been subjected to bombing by the enemy on several occasions but to date has suffered no losses in personnel or equipment."

4009th Quartermaster Truck Company

"This unit arrived in ——— Lancashire, England, on 28 January 1944. Was then moved to permanent station and its primary mission was to furnish necessary transportation for that District. This mission was carried out successfully until May 1944.

"Then the 4009th QM Truck Company was alerted for departure from the United Kingdom and sailed from a port in the United Kingdom, on D-Day, arriving off the coast of France on 7 June 1944, D plus 1, and immediately began disembarkation. By 8 June 1944, D plus 2, the complete unit had landed and was in operation.

"After working on beach clearance for a period of about one and one-half months, unit was placed on 'transportation' and then on detached service with the British Army in Belgium, where this unit helped supply the British drive into Holland. When this operation was completed, the unit was assigned to a Traffic Control point.

"We were re-assigned to beach clearance after completion of mission at the Traffic Control point until recent assignment to Seine Section, Communications Zone, where unit is part of the Motor Pool of the Seine Section.

"This organization participated in the Normandy Campaign, the Battle of Northern France, and the Battle of Germany. Unit was twice commended, once by Headquarters, European Theater of Operations, and once by Headquarters, 27th Army Group.

51st Army Postal Unit

"The 51st Army Postal Unit, consisting of eleven enlisted men and one officer, was activated on 27 December 1943, and reported to Camp Ellis on that date for a six weeks period of Unit Training.

"Having completed the required training, the Unit left Camp Ellis 16 February 1944 enroute to a port of embarkation. Following a brief but intensive period of preparation, and the subsequent journey, the —— APU arrived at its destination in England 10 March 1944.

"After acquiring the remainder of necessary equipment and completing the final stages of preparation, the Unit embarked for the Continent, arriving at the beach on D plus 23. Since that time APU —— has operated in the combat zone within reasonable proximity of the front lines, taking an important part in three major campaigns: The Invasion of the Continent, the Northern France Campaign, and the Invasion of Germany.

"At the present date APU —— is "Somewhere in Germany," having the distinction of being one of the first APO's operating east of the Siegfried Line. The personnel of this Unit is busy at the moment distributing Christmas mail to troops amid the sounds of heavy artillery, bursting shells, and the "putt-putt" of robot flying bombs overhead."

26th Hospital Train

"The 26th Hospital Train was activated at Camp Ellis, Ill., on the 10th of December, 1943. . . . On 5 May 1944, after inspection by post and Inspector General Department Officials, the unit was felt to be adequately trained for its mission overseas and was fortunate enough to be allowed the use and privilege of a Communications Zone type hospital train, for a brief period for familiarization.

"On 8 June 1944 five hospital trains were temporarily consolidated and shipped to the port of embarkation from which point we soon moved to the United Kingdom where we arrived on 30 June 1944.

"Soon after our arrival we were placed on detached service with the Seventh General Hospital. The officer and nurse personel functioned cohesively with the assigned personnel of the above hospital in the treatment of battle casualties. The enlisted personnel were distributed throughout the hospital, some working in the wards, others in the supply sections and still others aiding in the various administrative departments, as needed. This detached service continued up to 12 September 1944, when the unit was ordered to the 106th General Hospital. On 23 September 1944 United States Army Hospital Train No. 21 left an English port.

"On 30 September 1944 we arrived in Paris and were assigned to the Surgeon, Seine Section, Communications Zone, ETO. Since 20 October 1944, we have been detailed to evacuate battle casualties from field hospitals, evacuation hospitals, general hospitals, and other forward medical installations to rear area hospitals and occasionally to ports of debarkation.

"In carrying out our mission to date we have traveled approximately twenty thousand miles on the Continent and evacuated 9,264 battle casualties. In all this operation except for a few minor derailments the train has functioned without mishap until 23 December 1944, when a large enemy bomb exploded approximately thirty yards from the personnel cars, shattering all the windows and causing severe damage to all personnel quarters. Despite the marked damage to the cars we were able to continue evacuating battle casualties back to Paris before any repairs were started. Although personnel were badly shaken and shocked, no severe casualties resulted."

274th QM Bakery Company —Mobile Special

"The 274th QM Bakery Company left Camp Ellis on Decemer 18, 1943, for Camp Shanks, New York. After a short stay there, the company embarked for Liverpool, England, and arrived there safely on January 11, 1944.

"After several weeks in England, devoted to orientation and procurement of equipment, the 274th was divided into two separate organizations, which were designated the 3022nd and 3038th QM Bakery Company's Mobile (Special).

"The reorganization was followed by a short period of training in the use of British mobile bakery equipment. . . . Each organization was also provided a mobile coffee roaster, and several men trained in its operation.

"The company spent the next six months baking bread and roasting coffee for Quartermaster depots in England. Some two and a half million pounds of bread had been baked by the time the company was ready to leave for the Continent.

"On the 19th of August, the 3038th landed on the beach-head; after being set up in a number of places in France, the company became attached to the newly formed ——— U. S. Army, and arrived in Holland the 24th of October. Setting up only a few miles from the German border, it has thus far baked well over a million pounds of bread for the troops at the front. In spite of air raids and artillery shells landing nearby, production has not once been interrupted."

Letters from Individuals

From *Major* General *Henry S. Aurand (January, 1945), who commanded the 6th* Serv*ice Command from September,* 1942 *until the end of* October, 1944, *who writes from* France.

"The prize Sales Unit, QMC, is in Paris. I walked in and when I said 'General Aurand' they asked me to come back after work and talk to them. They trained at Ellis. General Littlejohn, who is Quartermaster here, and Colonel John Franks say: 'A grand job of training was done.' "

From *Lt. Col. Harrison S. Collisi, M. C., Commander,* 197*th* General *Hospital.*

My Dear Colonel Sullivan:

As Commanding Officer of the 197th General Hospital, I wish to thank you, sir, and the members of your staff, Colonel Butler, Colonel Bishop, Colonel Holcombe, Colonel Schull and Major Krakoff, for your very thoughtful Christmas Greeting Card from Camp Ellis.

Reaching us over here in France at a time when we have begun to profit by the excellent training and organization of our stay at Camp Ellis, we do certainly want you to know how much we appreciate it. Sincerely.

From *Lt. Col. Sidney* Pollock, 1301*st Engineer* G. S. *Regiment*

"Thought I would let you know how we are all doing. The three outfits that left together (the 1301st, 1303rd, and 1306th Engineer General Service Regts.), are all doing swell, and all making a good record. None of them have fallen down on a job. We all work for the Third Army, and in close contact with one another.

"Our men still talk of Ellis and say the war will never be as tough as Ellis. I hope they are right.

"All three of our outfits have had a few men pay the supreme price. I must say all the training we received in Ellis was O. K. and in line . . .

"Greetings to all of our friends who still remain."

From *Lt. Col. Glenn* J. *Jaoby, QMC, APO San* Francisco, *California*

"———— the best units I have seen in this whole area always seem to come from Ellis. The last does not only include QM units, but Medical and Engineer Units as well.

"All of the people I have talked to said that no matter how much '————' they did while they were at Ellis, they all were greatly appreciative of the fine training they received there.

"I am back now doing a little rehabilitating . . . I hope to get out of here on another operation soon. . . . This last operation I was on was most interesting and, from all appearances, the next one will outdo the last.

"With best regards to yourself and all the rest of the people there."

From *Major H. Sam* Francis, *QMC*

"Since we left Camp Ellis, our unit has done duty thus far on two different islands. I am sure you'd be interested to know I have encountered a few of your old Kansas State pupils here and there. It was a pleasure for me to be able to say I have done duty under you at Ellis, which gave me something in common with the men.

"At present our unit is handling the Labor situation for the island and you can rest assured we get plenty of activity night and day; however I hope this will be changed before long and we are headed for new places.

"My best wishes to you and my old commanding officer, Lt. Colonel Martin."

Features

THE personalities of Army camps differ, just as do those of the people who are a part and who guide the destiny of the camps. Ellis has many activities and special features that add to its personality in much the same way that its buildings and streets give it size and shape.

Within the limitations of space, the following pages tell the brief story of many of the camp's special features which include special services, sports, the Wacs, air-ground liaison, radio air target, garden project, the telephone system, Camp Ellis News, radio broadcasting, surrounding towns, the Red Cross, and the acknowledgments to the history's many contributors and workers.

Sports

CAMP ELLIS' accent on athletics has paid huge dividends in thrills to thousands of sports-loving soldiers and civilians during its short but action-filled history. From the day in May, 1943, when Lt. Robert Farmer, camp athletic officer, standing in mud up to the fourth buckle on his overshoes, welcomed candidates for the first Camp Ellis baseball team, until the present, sports have carved for themselves a special niche on the Ellis scene. Athletic competition, both camp-wide and intramural, has been given special attention and strong emphasis not only for its spectator interest but also for its value as a body-building, character-moulding instrument.

Familiar to many is the famous saying that the Battle of Waterloo was won on the playing fields of Eaton. Our country has thousands of "playing fields of Eaton" and can point with pride to the countless men in battle who a short time ago were the heroes of these playing fields—the men who not too long ago were hitting home runs, scoring touchdowns and field goals on the football fields, basketball courts, baseball diamonds and hockey rinks from the rugged Maine coastline to the peaceful California valleys. And Camp Ellis is proud to add its name to the long list of playing fields where youth battled for fun and glory before battling for life and liberty on more treacherous fields.

Far-sighted camp officials saw the need for a lusty athletic program and in every organization teams were organized, schedules drawn up and friendly rivalries ignited. This intra-unit program was in addition to the baseball, football, basketball and boxing activity organized to represent the post and provide thrills for the thousands who preferred the role of a spectator to that of a participant.

The caliber of teams that carried the colors of Camp Ellis and the athletes who participated ranked the camp aggregations with some of the most outstanding in the service. The parade of name-athletes who played both on camp and unit clubs has been endless. There were, for example, such sporting celebrities as Major Sam Francis, former Nebraska University football star; Lt. Ray Adams, former DePaul All-American basketball player, now serving as Camp athletic officer; "Sonny" Wood, ex-star of the New York Renaissance basketball team and selected on the All-World team; Pfc. Tom Draper, who pitched for the New York Giants against the Yankees in the 1927 World Series; Corp. William Broscovaki, former professional bike racer; Pvt. Ed Watkins, ex-Chicago Bear football player; Pvt. George Hamous, of Chicago's famed Sparta soccer team; Sgt. Albert Threadgill, one of the greatest high-jumpers in track

Bunker Hill tries a pass.

Gymnast experts perform.

Ellismen stop Ottumwa line smash.

Joe Louis visits Ellis.

Slugging it out.

history; Capt. Don Veller, former Indiana U grid star; Pfc. Bill Frazier, who pitched for the Chicago White Sox; Sgt. Roy Peeler, property of the Cincinnati Reds; "Bad Boy" Brown, popular pro wrestler; Staff Sgt. Robert Carpenter, former New York Giant pitcher; Pvt. Edward Boucy, 1943 intercollegiate tennis champion; Pvt. George Lake, property of the Detroit Tigers; Pfc. John Vrablik, catcher on the 1944 Camp Ellis team who was selected on the All-American semi-pro team for 1944, and from boxing circles such standouts as Cpl. Levi Southall, Cpl. William Gilliam, Sgt. Gene Joyce, Pfc. Vince Di Venti, Pvt. Matt Hammond, Sgt. Thomas Standifirl (Tommy Corbett) and Cpl. Costello (Cruz).

The greatest honor to come to Camp Ellis in the field of sports was the winning of the unofficial Army boxing championship by virtue of placing five men on the Chicago team which battled New York in Madison Square Garden in March of 1944. It was the first time in the 17-year-old history of Chicago-New York Golden Gloves that five men from any single center, city or camp were named to the team. Four of the boxers were able to make an appearance in the New York ring. Sgt. Gene Joyce was the only Ellis representative to score a victory. This achievement was not the only success accomplished by Camp Ellis in 1944. They commanded the spotlight again in September when they won the Sixth Service Command championship with five victories and one tie against formidable competition from Fort Custer, Mich., and Fort Sheridan and Camp Grant, Ill. A championship trophy was pre-

sented to Col. John S. Sullivan, Camp Commander, by Maj.-General Henry S. Aurand, Commanding General of the Sixth Service Command.

The biggest drawing card at Camp Ellis was the boxing exhibition staged by Sgt. Joe Louis and his troupe of Cpl. "Sugar Ray" Robinson, Pvt. Jack Wilson and Sgt. George S. Nicholson. The throng was estimated at 25,000.

Next in line of notable achievements was the record of the 1944 baseball team which closed its season in a blaze of glory by winning the Sixth Service Command title. A greater array of player talent, a more powerful schedule and a vastly improved record enabled the 1944 diamond troupe to surpass by far the mediocre season experienced by the 1943 club. Camp Ellis added the Service Command championship to its list of impressive records by defeating Gardiner General Hospital, 11 to 5, in the playoffs. Heavy hitting by all team members and a neat pitching trick by Sgt. Peeler, ace of the Cardinal staff, designed the victory. A recapitulation of the '44 season showed Ellis winning 33 games and losing eight. Peeler, property of the Cincinnati Reds, was the standout member of the squad. He pitched 18 victories and was defeated four times. In addition to his superlative mound work, Peeler captured the team batting championship with a .458 average.

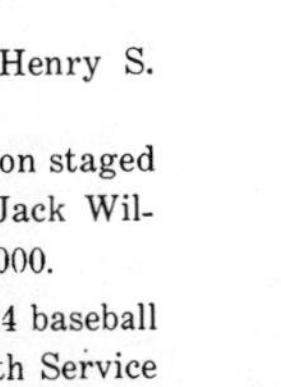

Some of the outstanding victories by Lt. Ray Adams' athletes were over the Minneapolis American Association, team and Camp Grant, Fort Custer and Mayo General Hospital. The Cardinals won 13 contests before their first defeat by a star-studded Camp McCoy team. Other laurels garnered by the Ellis club were an invitation to the National Semi-Pro tournament at Witchita, Kans., where the Ellis team reached the fourth round before being eliminated, winning the Illinois State Semi-Pro crown and registering a no-hit, no-run victory over Gardiner General Hospital.

Camp Ellis' first Post basketball team, 1943-44, was rated one of the powers in the midwest circles. Sparkplugs of the quintet which finished the season with 15 victories and nine defeats were Lt. Ray Adams, DePaul All-American and former professional star; Robert "Sonny" Wood, who previously played with the famous New York Renaissance and the World Champion Washington Bears, and "Whitey" Deinelt, formerly with the National Pro league Ft. Wayne (Ind.) Zollners. Wood, regarded as one of the classiest performers in basketball's history, was named on the 1944 all-World Professional selection of players.

Another successful season was written into the annals by the 1944-45 edition of the Ellis cagers. Main cogs on the machine which waded through a 25 game schedule with an impressive string of 20 victories were Robert Rogers and Tom Jaquet, both formerly of Oklahoma A & M varsity squads. The gem of the season proved to be a decisive 54-32 victory over Ottumwa, Ia., Navy, a team which defeated Camp Ellis, 56-45, in an earlier engagement. It was the first and only Ellis victory over a major Navy opponent in any sport. At this writing the Cardinals had the Sixth Service (Group I) Command title clinched, which would place them in a three-way battle for the Command title.

Bob Rogers, who took over the coaching of the 1944-45 team when Lt. Adams was transferred from camp at mid-season, broke the all-time Ellis individual scoring record, aggregating 344 points in 25 games. In victories and all-around balance, the 1944-45 squad was regarded as a stronger team than the 1943-44 quintet.

In conjunction with varsity inter-camp sports, Camp Ellis had a massive and varied intramural sports program which compared favorably with that of the largest military installations in the United States. There was never a dull moment in the Ellis sports realm. Baseball, touch-football, softball, basketball, boxing, horseshoe-pitching, badminton, bowling, tennis, archery and roller skating were conducted in a camp-wide program on a unit basis.

At its peak, Ellis had 184 softball teams playing in organized leagues which eventually lead to a Post tournament, the winner going to the Rock Island state tournament. Basketball at its height saw 224 teams playing in Quartermaster, Engineer and Medical Groups.

Tournaments were held to determine camp champions in all of nearly a dozen sports. Lack of bowling alleys did not hamper organization of leagues. Two eight-team enlisted men's leagues and one six-team officer league bowled weekly on the nearby Macomb alleys. In short, there was a maximum participation by military personnel in sports of all the four seasons of the year.

A recapitulation of Camp Ellis varsity records against out-of-camp competition shows Cardinal teams in seven sports participating in 179 matches winning 127 and losing 56, for a 75 per cent winning average. Broken down, the records show: Baseball: won 33, lost 8; basketball: won 35, lost 14; football: won 0, lost 5; boxing: won 50, lost 26; volleyball: won 1, lost 1; touch football: won 2, lost 1 and softball: won 0, lost 2.

Ellis also boasted its own trophy case which contained four awards. They included the Sixth Service Command baseball championship, the Sixth Service Command Boxing championship; the Peoria Golden Gloves Team boxing championship and the Illinois State Semi-Pro baseball championship.

Athletically speaking, the over-all program of Camp Ellis, considering it was one of the youngest military installations in the country, was one of the best, if not the best, and one of the most successful in the history of World War II.

Tense moment in Concordia game.

Jacquette scores for Ellis.

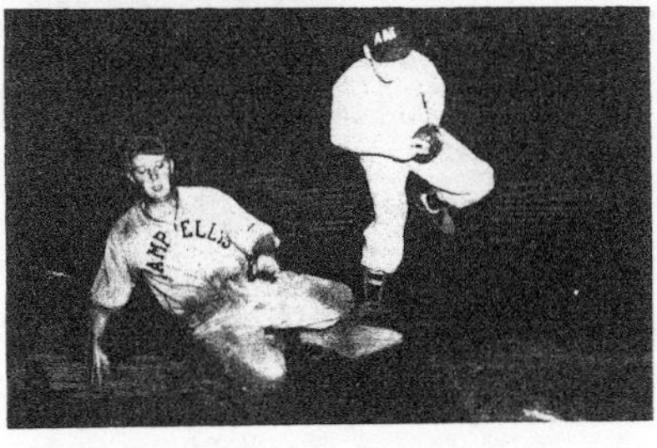

An Ellisman slides home.

Special Services

BEFORE Camp Ellis had outgrown the construction stage, a group of Sixth Service Command officers went into a huddle to formulate plans for the organization of a Special Service Section. They knew that when men were being trained to work and fight that their morale required the fullest opportunity of the complementary component of relaxation and were agreed that their program was to play a vitally important part in building that morale. By their enthusiasm, they gave assurances to Command officials that the soldiers of Camp Ellis would be provided with a comprehensive program of entertainment, recreation, educational guidance and amusement.

In mid April of 1943, Major Carson A. Hatfield arrived at Camp Ellis to head the Special Services Section. He was accompanied by Lt. Joseph Petrakovic who assisted in organizing the entertainment and recreational programs for the first troops to be stationed here. Two service clubs and two guest houses were soon put into operation and by the middle of the summer the last of six theaters had been opened.

In January, 1944, Major Ralph C. Manuel, post exchange officer, was appointed chief of Special Services. At that time the entire section was reorganized and under the jurisdiction of Special Services came the camp exchanges in addition to the athletic and recreational services, the libraries and the service club restaurants.

Entertainment

The soldiers of Ellis were never lacking for entertainment whether they were training in the camp proper or whether they were miles away fighting floods or making their bivouac encampments. Dances, band concerts, USO shows, all-soldier camp productions, company parties, roller skating and service club games provided those fun-seeking soldiers with a menu as appetizing as any to be found in the Sixth Service Command.

Of particular interest were the three all-soldier shows produced in camp; one of them, "By The Numbers," generally accepted by the soldiers as the greatest extravaganza presented, at the camp, played two performances nightly, Monday through Friday for two weeks and later "hit the road" playing to large audiences in the neighboring communities of Macomb, Lewiston, Galesburg and Springfield, the capitol city. Another, "Take A Break," played six times in the various recreation halls. The third, "My Busted Back,' a comical "take-off" on the soldier-in-training, though not played extensively, served as a medium to enable the soldier to laugh at himself.

Ellis soldiers were also entertained by radio, stage and screen stars and many bands which included those of Shep Fields, King Cole, Ada Leonard and Del Courtney. The Sixth Service Command All Star Show, under the direction of Major Wayne King, played to enthusiastic soldier-civilian audiences on two different occasions, and were entertained in turn by a party in their honor. Some of Hollywood's "he men" who came to camp, eating in GI mess halls and visiting and firing on the ranges, were Brian Donlevy and Charles Bickford. Movie-town "pin-ups" who set hearts to flutter were Shirley Deane and Lynn Merrick.

Theaters

As in civilian life the lure of the silver screen appealed to the thousands of soldiers training at Camp Ellis. Five months after the official opening of four theaters in various sections of the camp, the theater officer announced that the average attendance was 40,000 persons weekly. The first four theaters were opened on May 25, 1943. On June 12, the fifth theater opened while the sixth moviehouse to be constructed officially opened the following day.

Service to the Servicemen.

Lynn Merrick does K. P.

Nothing like a good book.

Ellis "Rockettes" in "By the Numbers."

Post Exchanges

During the first days of Ellis' occupancy soldiers purchased their cigarets and candy from an automobile which was being utilized as a mobile canteen. On April 12, 1943, the first exchange was opened and during the 12 hours it served the servicemen, a total of $17.54 was rung up on the cash register. Today the post exchange system is handling a business which runs into several million dollars and employs 363 civilians to operate the 16 GI "5 and 10's" and two restaurants.

"Service to the Servicemen" always has been the slogan of the Branch Exchanges at Camp Ellis and this motto was lived up to when mobile canteens followed Ellis soldiers to the flooded areas of southern Illinois where the soldiers fought rampaging waters for 24 hours daily.

Libraries

That a library is one of the favorite "hangouts" of a soldier during his spare time is evidenced in the fact that, according to library statistics, each soldier on the post paid at least one visit to one of the post's three libraries, and that one man in four borrowed a book. Special Services chiefs recognized that a well stocked library was a definite boost to the servicemen's morale and proceeded to pack the library shelves with all types of outstanding books.

When Camp Ellis' first library opened its doors on June 25, 1943, it was located on the second floor of the main service club and had a meager supply of 400 books. Today the library has its own barrack-type building and its shelves are lined with more than 5,000 books and its racks hold scores of magazines and newspapers from all sections of the nation. On October 12, 1943, a second library was opened on 43rd Street, while the patients' library was made ready at the Station Hospital in July of '43. This was strictly a bedside service and later expanded into a large reading room in the Red Cross building in the hospital area.

Bands

Talented musicians who in civilian days were members of such nationally famous orchestras as Ben Bernie, Sammy Kaye, Joe Venuti, Earl Hines, Isham Jones comprised the personnel of Camp Ellis' four major bands, namely, the Post Band, 343rd ASF Band, Training Group Band and Medical Group Band. The 343rd ASF Band was activated in November, 1943, and came to Camp Ellis from Des Plaines, Ill., where they served in a Military Police Battalion. In February, 1944, a nucleus of outstanding musicians came to this camp from Camp Perry, Ohio, and later formed the Training Group Band. Members of the Medical Group unit were former engineers at Ellis until September, 1944, when they were assigned to the Medical Group.

Brian Donlevy checking his score.

Wayne King and Bob Eberly entertain Ellismen

Ruth Terry entertains the patients.

Opening number in "Take a Break."

Air-Ground Liaison

CAMP ELLIS officials had forseen the need of Air-Ground Liaison Training as an important element in the thorough, realistic training of all troops. It was desired to provide the men with the most effective media in defense against air attack, understanding of tactics and employment of air power, methods of air-ground signal communication, effectiveness of camouflage as observed from the air, and the intelligent cooperation of troops with their air support. Immediate action was initiated to fulfill this need and the construction of an airfield was soon underway.

The first runway constructed at Camp Ellis, in early November, 1943, was completed in less than a day's time. More than a thousand Engineer troops went to work in the early morning and 23 hours later the gleaming metal-grid strip was ready to welcome the first detachment of four Stinson L-5 liaison planes. Two metal-grid landing strips were constructed, each approximately 5,800 feet long and 150 feet wide, thus providing Camp Ellis with an airfield to accommodate all types of aircraft. The facilities were constantly improved and the erection of an aircraft hangar was a proud addition. Air Corps Headquarters originally assigned the planes for a 30 day period, but the air-ground training was such an immediate success the Air Corps increased the detachment to seven planes manned by eleven pilots.

Original request for the aircraft to inaugurate the air-ground training program was made by the Training Division of Camp Ellis, and all activities and coordination of this training was placed under control of the Air-Ground Liaison Section of that division. All units were encouraged to employ this training aid at every opportunity on the basis that "Seeing is believing." An educational program was initiated for all units as a means of enabling them to employ the aircraft in the most intelligent and instructive manner, augmented by numerous field exercises with the aircraft in demonstrating the many phases they had previously studied. The use of aircraft proved to be a vital training aid to all unit commanders and key enlisted personnel as a means of aerial inspection of the performance of their unit. . . . getting a bird's-eye view and the realization of the extreme accuracy possible in aerial observation.

The Camp Ellis Air Detachment soon established itself by its activity in the skies. A great variety of missions was arranged to meet every requirement of this work with ASF troops. The liaison pilots stated they had never had such activity in all their flying days. The total missions would range from 40 to 150 flights per day with each plane averaging 6 flight hours per day . . . an extremely high average by any standard. These missions included observation of tactical road marches and convoys to note dispersion, intervals, and the efficiency of air alert system during simulated strafing attack; to observe the camouflage and discipline of units in bivouac and correct any mistakes; reconnaissance for bivouac sites and bridge crossings; performing air-ground signal communication by means of colored smoke grenades, panels, and message dropping and pick-up; aerial photos of unit field activity for group study by all personnel to note mistakes and measures necessary to correct them; flights by students of Post Camouflage School to observe all phases of camouflage constructed by them; these and many other types of missions found their place in the intensive training that has made the record of this camp so impressive. National interest centered on an errand of mercy performed by one of our planes when the Camp Commander dispatched an L-5 to Clinton, Iowa, to bring a noted brain surgeon here for an emergency operation on an injured soldier. Realism was the key-note at all times. Another feature provided to attain that end was the presence of P-39 and P-40 fighter aircraft here for a

The Stinson L-5

L 5 assimilates straffing attack.

Towing a target sleeve.

Constructing the Ellis air strip.

considerable time. They simulated strafing attacks so the troops could realize the high-speed and surprise possible with fighter aircraft. They also laid heavy smoke screens to simulate gas attacks. On two occasions 35,000 Ellismen witnessed a fire power demonstration performed by four B-25 bombers, four P-39's and four P-40's from the 2nd Composite Squadron. This demonstration gave the troops a sample of the "real thing," medium and low altitude bombing, using 250-lb. and 500-lb. bombs, laying smoke screen, strafing of silhouette tank targets, using .50 cal. and 37 mm. shells, and the speed and surprise that is possible in air attack.

The successful record of the air-ground training program has well justified its place in the training of ASF troops at Camp Ellis in providing them with the confidence that is instilled by the "know how."

Radio Air Target

ANOTHER training feature at Camp Ellis was the .50 caliber Anti-Aircraft Training Program introduced by the Training Division in the spring of 1944.

The assigned personnel received special training at Fort Sill, Oklahoma in the maintenance and operation of the 24 small scale radio-controlled planes which were used as targets. The range was located at Dunes Park, Zion, Ill., where the shoreline of Lake Michigan provided a safe area for firing the .50 caliber anti-aircraft guns.

The planes were launched from a catapult which sent them into the air at 60 miles an hour. The pilot, seated at the radio control on the ground, maneuvered the plane through antics assimilating actual combat flying—climbing, turning, diving—ever attempting to outsmart the gunners who were trying to knock his ship from the skies.

A battery of eight .50 caliber anti-aircraft machine guns were fired at the planes with tracer bullets to guide the gunners' aim. At first the soldiers experienced difficulties in getting the range on the small, fast-moving targets, but after a few days they began to score a heavy percentage of hits.

Ellis flood fighters relax to read the "News."

Camp Ellis News

MUCH of the history of Camp Ellis has been told in the pages of its newspaper, the Camp Ellis News, a sober and rather stiff-collared weekly that shuns the flamboyancy of other service periodicals. Its policy has been to let the news tell itself and to allow its readers to judge accordingly.

The first issue, appearing eight days after the station complement cadre arrived, was a modest, pint-sized mimeographed edition. Only a temporary expedient, the mimeographed paper became a 4-page printed tabloid two weeks later. It was printed on the presses of the Macomb Journal, in Macomb, Ill., where it has been published ever since.

As the camp swelled, the number of pages grew to 16 and for one week the camp boasted a 20 page paper. Considered the largest Army paper published without the benefit of advertising, the News had a 13,700 circulation during its peak runs.

In February, 1944, the News was entered in a national contest conducted by the University of Missouri to determine the best Army paper published in this country. The News was rated among the first six.

Wacs are guests of Ellis radio show.

Radio Broadcast

CAMP ELLIS is the only Army Installation in the U. S. proper with its own radio network. Through this medium, news and entertainment originating from the camp reaches an estimated 200,000 listeners weekly. However, like every successful enterprise, it took foresight, imagination and plain doggedness, to accomplish this goal.

When the camp opened, the Public Relations Office organized a radio department to acquaint the people of Central Illinois with its training mission. For a number of months, daily 15-minute shows, were broadcast from the studios of nearby stations.

In November of 1943, the first show originating from camp was broadcast from Service Club No. 1 by remote control through station WMBD in Peoria. It was a dignified program of concert music, violin and piano recitals. But the camp was hep and the clamor for more jump and jive prevailed. Talent on the post was scouted and used on the show. Two months later five other stations WJBC Bloomington, WGIL Galesburg, WTAX Springfield, WMBF Rock Island, and WSOY Decatur, joined the network. It wasn't long before the show's opening catch words "Camp Ellis Entertains" became a listening habit at 8:00 every Tuesday night.

They marched from the train.

Eating their first chow at Ellis.

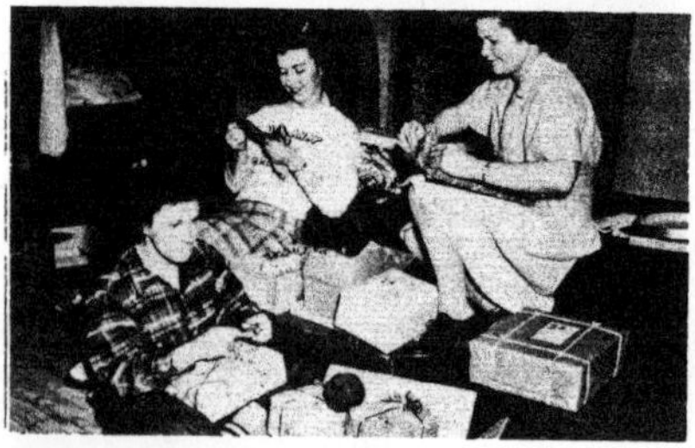

Opening Christmas presents.

WACS relax.

The Wacs

WOMEN in the Army was still rather new to the male side of the military picture when the first Wac contingent bounced daintily into camp in January, 1944, and set up housekeeping in specially built barracks with indoor plumbing. They agreed unanimously that Ellis was a far-cry from the creature comforts of Fort Brady, whence they came, but like good soldiers they came prepared for every eventuality.

The majority of the women had served at Fort Brady, Mich., for many months, and were well acquainted with Army routine. They were experienced in company organization, close order drill and every woman had received training in some technical service. They came prepared to work and within a day of their arrival most of them were on their new jobs. Assigned here to replace soldiers for overseas duties, the changeover took longer than originally anticipated, but before many weeks were up headquarters soldiers were on their way to overseas training units.

Despite the mid-winter bleakness of

their first days in camp, the Wacs found much warmth in the camp's social life. It did not take Ellismen long to decide that the distaff side of the Army was an attractive innovation. The Wac bulletin board was soon crowded with invitations from many of the units on the post. The neighboring cities and towns offered a variety of entertainment.

Spring was late that year, but love interest prospered despite the weather. The camp chaplain was kept quite busy knotting the ties of matrimony between soldiers and their female counterparts. No count was ever kept of the number of Wac marriages, but the score was astonishingly conclusive that women lose none of their glamor in uniform.

Of particular interest is the fact that two Camp Ellis Wacs, utilizing the skill they brought to the Army, were assigned as telephone operators for the famous Roosevelt-Churchill Conference at Quebec, Canada, in Sept., 1944.

Scores of the original cadre that came here are now serving overseas and several have received commissions. Early skeptics who questioned the practicality of women in the Army became their staunchest supporters when they were able to see for themselves the quality of work they were performing.

A couple of nice numbers.

A Wac at her work.

Giving a fellow GI the needle.

Victory Garden

AN EXPERIMENT viewed with a great deal of professional interest and personal satisfaction by Camp Ellis' farming neighbors was the large scale victory garden begun in the early spring of 1944.

Two hundred acres of rich soil adjacent to the highway and not easily adaptable for training was set aside for the project. A select group of soldiers experienced in farming prepared and planted the soil which had lain idle for over two years.

The first seeding included early April potatoes, spinach, radishes, beets, turnips, peas, lettuce, carrots, onions, and parsley. The later plantings consisted of the different varieties of beans and corn, cabbage, and other vegetables that have a longer growing season.

The final amazing yield of 525,825 pounds of more than 30 varieties of vegetables exceeded the expectations of even seasoned Illinois farmers. The heaviest crop was tomatoes, 95 tons; followed by green beans, 38 tons; corn, 35 tons; squash, 25 tons; cucumbers, 21 tons; and sweet potatoes, 19 tons.

The "field to table" economy proved so successful that in addition to the $58,000 estimated value of the crop, and its noteworthy contribution to the total wartime food supply, the project brought to Camp Ellis' mess halls many vegetables otherwise unobtainable on the open market.

Red Cross

MORE than 25,000 Ellismen brought their personal and family problems to the American National Red Cross since it began operation at Ellis on April 26, 1943. Home conditions, reports to support requests for emergency furloughs and discharges, re-establishment of contact between servicemen and their families, and financial aid to soldiers and their dependents were daily routine to the Field Director and his assistants. In the 22-month period 4,085 loans and grants amounting to $108,592.39 were made at the camp.

Thousands of G I Patients at the Station Hospital were kept in good spirits by the recreational facilities provided by the Red Cross. Those who were up and about spent many hours in the recreation building where they were entertained with movies, shows, parties, games, and provided with recreational facilities of all kinds. The volunteer "Gray Ladies" went to the bedside of the others, distributing magazines, games, radios, comfort items, refreshments and letter writing supplies.

More than 150 men and women have been sent to Camp Ellis from National Red Cross Headquarters in Washington, D. C., for training to qualify for overseas assignments. The work of nurses' aides, making of surgical dressings, and first aid courses are other Red Cross programs which have operated

The heart of the telephone system.

The operators line up for chow.

A garden spot in the center of the Camp.

Operators live in three dormitories.

Telephone Company

KNOWN as "Camp Spoon River" when the Illinois Bell Telephone Company started its service during the early stages of construction, Camp Ellis grew within a year into a communication nerve center with 35 switchboard positions and service for 1,000 lines.

Illinois Bell construction crews set poles and strung wires across many miles of central Illinois. They crossed and re-crossed territories served by smaller, independent telephone companies, which were co-operating to speed the job.

Four branch telephone centers, with operators in attendance, handle the heavy long-distance traffic during the hours that soldiers are free from duty. More than forty miles of cable are connected to a major Chicago-St. Louis toll line at Mason City, Ill., making Ellis toll service speedy and efficient.

The operators, who live and work in a centrally located area at 35th and S Streets, are comfortably housed in three girls' dormitories. This fact, along with the combination switchboards the girls operate for calls and toll service, makes Camp Ellis one of only four installations in the country with this unusual method of handling service.

Surrounding Towns

MOST of the cities and towns surrounding Camp Ellis were unknown to the thousands of soldiers who trained here. During their training period they became acquainted with the habits and customs of their new neighbors, and their neighbors in turn became acquainted with soldiers who were gathered here from every state in the union.

The nearby towns most frequently visited by the soldiers were Peoria, Springfield, Pekin, Canton, Lewistown, Havana, Beardstown, Quincy, Ipava, Table Grove, Macomb, Bushnell and Galesburg. As the camp grew in size, USO clubs were set up in all these cities and towns to guide the soldiers to suitable places of entertainment.

Red Cross drives, War Bond campaigns and other patriotic meetings were supplied with speakers and entertainers chosen by the Public Relations Office from among the talented personnel of Camp Ellis.

The camp was always open to visitors and during its early months the camp saw thousands of visitors come and go. War veterans and other patriotic groups took a personal interest in the camp and contributed day room equipment and other entertainment items for the welfare of the soldiers.

USO, Havana, Ill.

Snack Bar, Macomb USO.

Girls entertain at Canton USO.

Thanksgiving Dinner, Table Grove USO.

Acknowledgements . . .

The historical research section has done an excellent and painstaking job in this narrative story of Camp Ellis. The book, which comprises more than two years of the camp's active history, spans a period of the nation's most crucial days. The history of Camp Ellis is thus intimately related with the progress of the war.

Those who worked on this book have put in long hours and months of hard labor. Their reward is the finished book which in itself reflects the effort that went into its production.

The officer in charge of the project was Capt. Robert O. Burton, who supervised the compiling of editorial matter, the design, lay-out, art work, and the printing of the book.

The writing of the book, which was started by T/Sgt. Edgar H. Semprini and Corp. Tyler M. Hurt, was completed by T/4 John G. Buvens and T/4 Arthur L. Massolo, when the former were transferred to other stations.

Design, layout and lettering was done largely by T/3 Elmer T. Lehnhardt. His ideas were later carried through by T/4 Ray Jansma when Sgt. Lehnhardt was transferred. He was assisted by Pfc. Robert D. Hantz. Pfc. Charles G. Torosian was responsible for some of the illustrations.

Sgt. John C. Reynolds supervised the mechanical production of the book. T/4 Robert G. Galinski was in charge of the press work and was assisted by T/5 Robert L. Dozier. T/4 James W. Reilley and T/4 John T. Maher did the photo-lithograph work. The entire body type of the book was set on a Linotype by Pfc. Hubert E. Post. Final press proofs were printed by T/4 James W. Reilley and Sgt. Carl F. Wallace.

Many days were spent in the selection of the pictures which illustrate the book. Thanks is owed to the camp's Signal Corps Photo Laboratory and the photo section of the Engineer and Medical Groups for cooperating with the editors.

The picture of the "Old Mill" in the Bernadotte section of the history was lent to the editors by Mr. Lachlan Crissey of Lewistown, Ill.

For advice and helpful assistance gratitude is extended to the Camp Public Relations Office and the Macomb Daily Journal, where the type composition was made.

Appreciation is extended to all the groups, divisions and sections for submitting material which assisted the editors in writing the book.

JOHN S. SULLIVAN,
Colonel Infantry,
Commanding.

Spotted something that isn't quite right?

Let us know and we'll fix it for future reprints. And as a thank you for your diligence, we'll send you a free Sothis book of your choice.

publisher@sothis.press

This page intentionally left blank

Made in United States
Orlando, FL
06 November 2026

90301609R00079